THE
REIKI
GUIDE

THE REIKI
GUIDE

A Journey of Transformation

SAM GODDARD

"Red Feather Mind Body Spirit Feather" logo is a
registered trademark of Schiffer Publishing, Ltd.

Design by Insight design concepts ltd.
Type set in Neutra text/Aspergit

ISBN: 978-0-7643-6380-1
Printed in India

Published by REDFeather Mind, Body, Spirit
An imprint of Schiffer Publishing, Ltd.
4880 Lower Valley Road
Atglen, PA 19310
Phone: (610) 593-1777; Fax: (610) 593-2002
Email: Info@redfeathermbs.com
Web: www.redfeathermbs.com
For our complete selection of fine books on this
and related subjects, please visit our website at
www.redfeathermbs.com. You may also write
for a free catalog.

Contents

Introduction

If I skipped back twenty years to when I was first introduced to Reiki, I couldn't have imagined what a huge impact it would have on my life. I am constantly humbled by the profound guidance and trust that Reiki energy can offer anyone who is called to explore this energetic system in further depth, and how learning Reiki can so often be just the beginning.

I am privileged to have worked for many years with Reiki across various industries and assisted hundreds of individuals on their own Reiki paths. Now I am guided to share my experience of this incredible tool and journey with you through the pages of this book.

I feel that we are living in a time when we understand that taking ownership of our own well-being is a prerequisite to a healthy and happy life; not only for ourselves, but also for our families. We are being called to heighten our awareness of self-care and, on a deeper path, self-mastery, in order to bring balance into what has become for most of us, such a demanding and often-ungrounding pace of life. I believe that Reiki is the perfect tool to offer that balance, whether it is for ourself or for our children.

Although Reiki is often referred to as a healing modality, my own experience over the years has led me to believe that calling it such is actually very limiting, since it can offer so much more. It has been known to benefit anyone, from a baby inside a mother's womb to a person at the end of their life and pretty much everyone and everything in between. I have worked with an incredibly varied clientele and student base over the years and have been witness to the most cynical of people awakening to the possibilities found in making subtle shifts in perception of the world and our place within it. My Reiki journey is one of duality: first, that of healing and assisting myself, and then supporting others to move away from a purely logical and head-driven way of seeing life, and to drop into a place of intuition, connection, and feeling.

It is my intention to relay my own experience of life with Reiki as a tool for everyday living, as well as exploring from a broader perspective the potential benefit of growing our energetic awareness on all levels. In my experience, Reiki can indeed be a wonderful system to support us in that growth, from whatever age we find ourselves drawn to explore.

As a mother of a ten-year-old boy, I am passionate about teaching moms and moms-to-be about Reiki—how they can use it for themselves, in the home, and with their offspring/children. In an age when kids are being influenced to such a degree by technology, social demands, and comparison to others, I feel it is essential to offer them a choice of alternative skill sets to help empower and balance their childhood and adolescence.

Reiki as an energetic system has a natural crossover with other empowering holistic tools that I will reference throughout this book, including mindfulness, crystals, essential oils, sound, color, and many more. My own journey has led me to study and practice many holistic, shamanic, and spiritual modalities, since I find Reiki is often a catalyst to open further doors of exploration. Some of the information may resonate—some may not. This is purely an invitation to be open-minded to these ancient tools and systems—an opportunity, should you wish

to take it—to gather some time for yourself and to honor your inner knowledge of what is right for you at any given time.

For many, the prospect of exploring these systems may mean a jump into the unknown and very often a sense of resistance to what we perceive "that world" to be. If you notice this sense rise in you, then—if possible—I invite you to remove the labels that have been placed upon these systems in your experience, and approach this book with what is referred to in mindfulness practice as the "new mind." Allow any preconceived knowledge and judgment to be placed to one side: let the energy of this offering be a new experience and possibility.

Since I started learning Reiki, many systems have evolved and been channeled by numerous masters across the world. This has meant that there are now over a hundred different systems of how to teach and share Reiki. I feel this is inevitable, since I don't believe that "one size fits all." Reiki is constantly evolving, as are we. I believe that everyone is called to the right teacher, and the right system, at the right time, and as long as it is taught with integrity and honor, the student will be supported and guided. This does not negate my passion about the morality of how Reiki is taught and the importance of honoring the origins of the Usui Reiki system, but allows for inclusivity and fluidity.

I wish to be clear that the opinions that I share in this book about Reiki are mine and are born through my experience. They are not intended as a definitive set of "how to" instructions, but a gentle invitation and guidance to support you on your own exploration. How you receive this offering is, of course, your choice. I am conscious that there may well be established Reiki masters who may not agree with everything I say. However, I feel that is an important point: the beauty of Reiki energy is that it supports, enlightens, and empowers us, in our own individual process. The chapters that follow are an offering of my personal experience, my passion, and my feelings about how Reiki can be the most precious gift to support us in life—however and whenever it knocks on our door.

For my part, I hope to share the very real and practical nature of Reiki and the empowering tools that are available to all of us. And to offer you a hand in finding the bridge that is right for you to consciously cross in your own time and at your own pace, with both feet firmly on the ground. There is no magic power required to do so, no special gift that is found in only a few. It is my experience that when we start to open to a more energetic view of life, we simply start to remember what we already know on some deeper level. Anyone can do this—it is not exclusive; it is a matter of choice.

行 journey

MY JOURNEY SO FAR

My journey so far

I used to believe I could fly: I still do on some level. I remember this fact being awakened in me in a training-room environment one day, when someone else mentioned this phenomenon they had experienced as a child, and it all came flooding back. Well, when I say flooding, more snippets of memories of me leaving my body and flying around my bedroom and garden.

But nevertheless, it was real.

I then started to remember other elements of sensitivity as a child, not wanting to go into certain buildings, having a real sense that I didn't "belong" in school. Finding it on many levels easier to converse with my teachers, rather than my peers. Being able to pick up on other people's feelings from a very early age. All of this was somewhat locked away from my accessible memories after, shall we say, my "colorful" and often-traumatic teenage years, which led to a sustained period of panic attacks and disconnection to that knowledge and those memories.

I sought connection as a young adult through traveling, music, and dancing. These were my loves, my passions, my opportunities to escape much hidden internal pain. Pain from the split of my parents as an only child; the complicated, often-terrifying and ungrounded life of living with an alcoholic mother; and the fierce feeling inside that there had to be more to life and, more importantly, my life.

Due to my unsettled circumstances, I had already become incredibly independent, so it was no real shock to friends and family when in my early twenties I decided to travel the world on my own. This sense of freedom has something that I have always relished, a rawness that I revel in. I found beautiful unpredictability in unplanned travel, living outside the known and trodden pathway, and embracing the new.

The memories of that trip and many others before and after remain emblazoned in my heart far more than my mind, since even then I believe I was beginning to understand the authentic space of experience, rather than intellectual analysis. The people I have met over the years, the often-brief but spectacular encounters I have been privileged to have with individuals, places, and animals: all of these no doubt contribute to what happened next.

It was many years later, while sitting in my office on 56th Avenue, New York, working as a director of market planning for a financial management company, that it hit me—this is not for me. I had worked hard, recognized, and snapped up opportunities that had revealed themselves, and at the age of twenty-seven was doing rather well, thank you. Good job, great salary, part-time student at Columbia University, and a flat in Hell's Kitchen. I was the quintessential work-hard, play-hard gal from London.

Yet, I was also acutely aware that there was something else at play. I noticed how in my work, I was continuously surrounded by incredibly stressed people, pressure, and projection. Yes, like many others I could play the game, but underneath there was still that hole one feels. I had tried to fill that hole the best way I knew by immersing myself in the creative wonder of New York and going to as many gigs, galleries, and parties as possible. It was during this time that I met some incredibly talented musicians and artists who could "see" this hole in me and asked whether I had ever considered creative management. Simultaneously, and no doubt serendipitously, it seemed that every time I was out and open, there was one word that kept entering my periphery: Reiki.

I would hear it in conversations in bars, notice it in magazines; it was almost as if the word itself was whispered on the very winds that carried me through that time. Those whispers began to get louder until it was almost deafening, and I knew I had to do something about it.

My mother was not well, I knew I was not happy in my job, and it was time to go home. So I gave it all up (as many referred to it) and headed back to London, with no job and soon no money. Pretty much the first thing I did was call my mother to see how she was feeling. She and I had our differences over the years, but there was always a lot of love between us, despite it being hidden through some of the darker years. She mentioned to me how she had been having this amazing treatment from a local lady she had been introduced to, and that it seemingly was the only thing that was helping her health. On hearing this I said, "Let me guess—is it called Reiki?" Her answer confirmed the inevitable.

I asked if I could see her "Reiki lady," not even knowing how to address someone who "did" Reiki at that time, and she made an appointment for me.

That "her" turned out to be a wonderful, wise, and ultimately incredibly influential lady called Jackie Rees, a Reiki master living in Kent. She came to visit and held a Reiki session for me, and the rest, as they say, is history. As clichéd as it sounds, it was as if all my questions and searching over the years came flooding into that one session, with a simple answer of "this is your path."

The years that followed saw my interest in Reiki turn into a passion, and it remains so today. I have been fortunate to be able to follow that path on a glorious and unpredictable journey of self-mastery and, ultimately, service to others. It has not, and as I understand will not ever pretend to be, an easy path, yet my calling to Reiki and its many gifts continues to astound me and remains one that I will be forever grateful for.

Reiki has supported my work across many industries, including the music industry, corporate life, and event management. It has guided me to assist countless souls on their journeys through my private work and through my schools. Yet ultimately, it always comes back to my own journey. I often tell this story in various lengths when I teach Reiki, not to embrace my ego but to, I hope, illuminate the fact that I truly believe Reiki is beneficial to anyone, anywhere, and at anytime. This is the beauty of Reiki, of energetic connection, of connection to Source: it is limitless, as are we.

秤
balance

BALANCE IS THE KEY

Balance is the key

People often ask me, "What is Reiki?" After all this time, I still find myself pausing before I answer the question. My usual go-to response is that it is an energy therapy rather than perhaps the more popular response of a form of healing. There are a couple of reasons I choose to refer to it as an energy therapy. First, I am conscious of using the word "healing" in relation to Reiki; yes, it has been known to have incredible healing results, and of course there is the healing element to working with Reiki. However, to me, healing implies that somehow the practitioner heals a client by a kind of transference of his or her own magical healing powers. However, the truth is that a Reiki practitioner actively facilitates an individual to heal themselves by learning to channel universal life force energy: *ki*. The second reason is that to define Reiki in a single sentence or as a single act is not only very difficult but also very limiting.

In truth, my feeling is that Reiki is an incredibly empowering tool to help us bring balance to our life, be that on a physical, emotional, or spiritual level, and in many cases, all three. Most of us spend a lot of our time leaning into one of these elements of self. Perhaps we have had a lot of physical issues in our life, or we are suffering with our mental and emotional health, or maybe we are so tired of battling in both of these areas that we decide to choose a spiritual path and free ourselves of it all. The fact is that what will bring us the optimum healthy and happy life is a homeostasis between the three: balance.

This simple triangle model shows what I feel Reiki can offer, and reminds us of the intrinsic nature of self. More often than not, on reflection of this model comes the familiar nod of resonance, when we realize how our lives can be so easily out of balance and how our focus on one level of being can directly influence another.

In purely energetic terms, I like to compare it to our blood circulation, in that we want it to flow to its optimum potential. We wouldn't want to have a blood clot of any kind, and in fact we naturally do our utmost to keep our blood circulation as healthy as possible. It's the same in regard to our energetic system—we need to keep it flowing as well as possible. Unfortunately, what often happens is that blocks are created due to ill health and trauma, and these blocks can cause us to become unbalanced, ungrounded, and ultimately unhappy.

We all have trauma in our life at one stage or another and perhaps also in previous lifetimes, depending on one's belief. For now, it's important to note that for the purpose of this book, when I refer to the word "trauma" and the energy attached to it, this can mean anything from stubbing your toe to a war zone and everything that falls between. Our trauma is relevant, no matter where it started. Of course, with deeper levels of trauma, there are often deeper energetic blocks that are embedded within our systems and bodies.

People are complex beings that have a multitude of layering in behavior and beliefs, but we also have choice. We can be empowered to choose to bring healing to ourselves by working with Reiki. A higher vibrational universal energy that we can learn to channel in order to bring light, and ultimately shifts to those areas of darkness, rigidity, and behaviors that no longer serve us.

We do this by learning to put our unevolved ego aside and literally get out of the way, so that the pure vibrational and intelligent energy we are channeling can do its job. For many, this element of getting out of the way and not necessarily needing to return to the trauma to heal it, is a wonderful alternative to some other forms of trauma-related work.

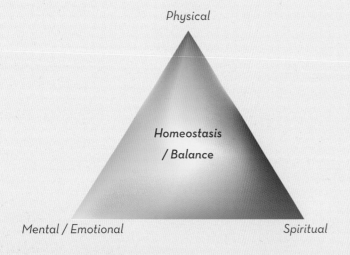

Physical

Homeostasis / Balance

Mental / Emotional　　*Spiritual*

The fact that we are literally made up of energy on a cellular level and therefore have a vibration, can help us understand the idea of connecting to a higher vibrational Source. It can also help us understand that we are undeniably connected to every living thing and that some form of energy exchange is happening every moment of every day, whether we choose to be awake to it or not.

I was lucky enough to meet a kaminchu a few years ago at a water ceremony and blessing. A kaminchu is an Okinawan shaman and a female oracle, from an ancient and gifted group of women who channel information from the divine. This particular kaminchu, Kazumi Ohishi, had broken tradition and decided to travel the world to share her message in relation to how we can help our planet. While sitting listening to this incredible, white-robed woman in a small, unassuming room in Somerset, it was her words around vibration that really struck me. She had much to say, but it was when she explained through her beautiful Japanese translator that we have one task in life, and that is to raise our vibration and grow, that I really responded. She continued to say that if we didn't know what she meant by "raise our vibration," she was referring to those times when we step outside in the sunshine and see the most-beautiful flowers or butterflies and feel a flutter deep within our hearts. That, she said, is raising your vibration.

Our tendency in today's society is to complicate matters, to assume that the more difficult systems and techniques are to understand, that somehow the more beneficial they must be. One of the reasons I love Reiki is that it is so simple. I have always said that the complication of Reiki is its simplicity. Of course, not all would agree, and some have indeed placed a lot more rigidity and rules on Reiki than I personally feel is necessary. I believe working with Reiki is a simple matter of choice, honor, and truth, and if you like, tapping into something that on some level we already know how to do.

Life is simply spent remembering what the soul already knows

—*Salma Farook*

Our chakra system

In Western Reiki, the chakra system is often used as a focus for our practice.

The word chakra come from Sanskrit and translates to wheel or disk, but it refers to a spiritual energy center within the human body. It is said that the chakra system is referenced in the *Vedas*, the earliest Sanskrit literary records and most-ancient scriptures of Hinduism. Therefore, for centuries the chakra systems have been a focus in yoga and meditation—the intention being to stimulate and ensure a healthy energetic system, open and aligned. This encourages the flow of *prana* or, as we call it in Reiki, *ki*, thus keeping us healthy, vibrant, and essentially balanced.

These energy centers can be thought of as the basis of the human energetic structure and influence our physical and emotional states. They register the harmony of the physical, emotional, and spiritual health of the individual.

Reiki is a powerful balancing force for the chakras when they become blocked or stagnant and prevent the healthy flow of energy. Imbalances in the chakras are also referred to as energy blocks.

Most commonly, seven main chakras are identified from your root to the crown of your head. The lower chakras relate to earthly matters such as survival, sex, and empowerment. In contrast, the higher chakras relate to our higher consciousness, truth, intuition, and purpose. Our heart chakra, which bridges the two, governs empathy, love, and compassion.

There is a huge amount of information and exploration that can be looked for in relation to our chakra system. As always, I would encourage an initial pathway of simplicity and then layer that pathway with experience and further study. Inevitably on further investigation—depending on the route you choose—there is often variance in depiction. Here is a basic overview including color, purpose, and position, as well as some of the corresponding crystals.

First chakra

Position: Between the legs, between the genitals and the anus
Name: Root/Muladhara
Purpose: Governs physical needs, security, and grounding
Color: Red
Crystals: Garnet, ruby, red jasper, and tiger's eye

Second chakra

Position: The sacral, which is about two fingers in width beneath the navel
Name: Sacral/Svadhishthana
Purpose: Governs sexuality, emotions, creativity, and desires
Color: Orange
Crystals: Carnelian, orange jasper, sunstone, and coral

Third chakra

Position   Just beneath the waist
Name: Solar plexus/Manipura
Purpose: Governs power
Color: Yellow
Crystals: Topaz, citrine, and amber

Fourth chakra

Position: Area of the heart
Name: Heart center/Anahata
Purpose: Connects and governs love, forgiveness, and compassion
Color: Green
Crystals: Emerald, green tourmaline, green calcite, and rose quartz

Fifth chakra

Position: The throat
Name: Throat/Vishuddha
Purpose: Governs communication and ability to speak our truth
Color: Light blue
Crystals: Turquoise, blue topaz, and blue lace agate

Sixth chakra

Position: Between the eyebrows
Name: Third eye/Ajna
Purpose: Governs intuition and reasoning
Color: Indigo
Crystals: Amethyst, pearl, sapphire, and lapis lazuli

Seventh chakra

Position: Crown of the head
Name: Crown/Sahasrara
Purpose: Governs spirituality and connection to our higher selves and the Divine
Color: White/gold
Crystals: Diamond, gold, and clear crystal quartz

Chakra

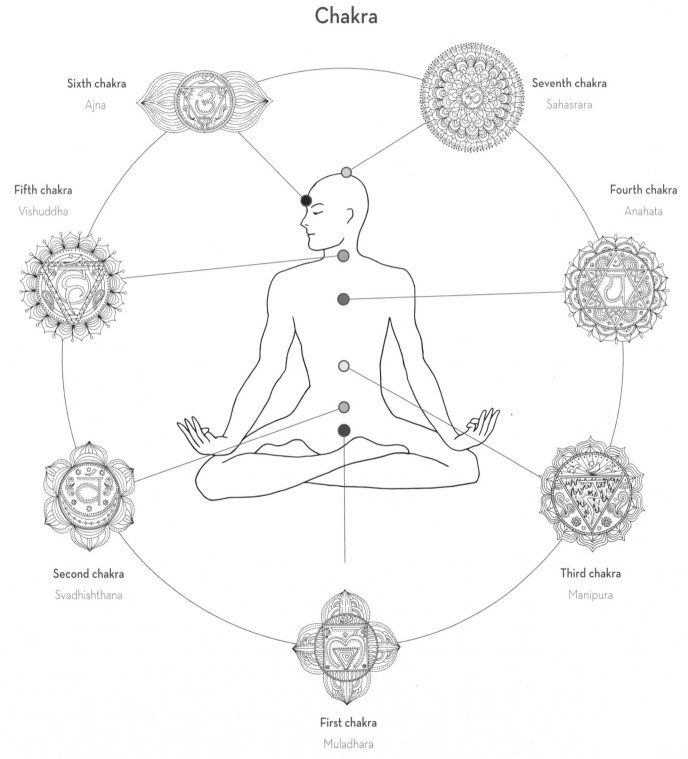

Sixth chakra
Ajna

Seventh chakra
Sahasrara

Fifth chakra
Vishuddha

Fourth chakra
Anahata

Second chakra
Svadhishthana

Third chakra
Manipura

First chakra
Muladhara

Feeling energy

1. This is a simple exercise referred to as the "Energy Ball," which can help us become accustomed to the tangibility of the energy around us, our aura.

2. Find a comfortable position seated in a chair, with your feet flat on the ground.

3. When you are ready, close your eyes and hold your arms out in front of you, shoulder width apart, with your fingers closed and your palms facing one another.

4. Breathe and begin to focus on the space between your palms. As you do so, very gently and slowly begin to move your palms toward each other, the intention being to focus on any sensations or observations you may notice as you move your hands together. This is to invite a sense of curiosity and openness.

5. You may begin to feel some tingling, warmth, and even some resistance, almost as if you are pushing through or against something. Continue to move your hands until you are about 4 in. (10 cm) apart and then hold this position and, again, just notice.

6. After a while, you may wish to move your hands farther apart and again bring them together and see if you can gauge an increase in feeling.

7. So, what are you feeling? Energy.

8. With practice, you may begin to feel into the edges of a ball shape as you bring your hands toward each other. If you are able to feel this, then I'd invite you to play with your ball of energy and see what is possible. In addition, you may also feel changes in temperature or weight.

9. If you have trouble feeling anything, perhaps start by rubbing your palms together vigorously for about one minute. Now try again. Everyone is different.

10. In addition to this exercise, you can try working with a friend or on a pet to try to sense the energy field around them. Don't be disheartened if this is challenging; relax and try again.

霊気 reiki

REIKI—
AN ANCIENT SYSTEM
FOR MODERN TIMES

Reiki—an ancient system for modern times

As I have already mentioned, I believe there to be over a hundred different systems of Reiki that are taught across the world, and it is my feeling that whatever system you are drawn to is the "right" system for you. When I say system, I have heard this referred to also as style, type, or even branch. I am referring to a way in which Reiki is taught by a specific master, school, or organization.

My own Reiki journey, in terms of study, started with Usui Reiki and has evolved over the years to include Usui/Tibetan Reiki, Karuna Reiki®, Holy Fire Reiki®, Reiki Drumming™, and an openness to explore whatever system I am called to. This does not diminish my honoring of my original lineage to Usui Sensei and the Usui Reiki teachings, which are still a large part of what I am guided to teach today. However, my feeling is that Reiki evolves, as do we, and therefore there is an inevitability of change, evolution, and differing ways of developing, delivering, and exploring what is ultimately our connection to Source energy, love, and subsequent healing.

I heard a beautiful analogy recently: that the delivery of Reiki is like a language, and there are hundreds of languages throughout the world. Reiki for me is Reiki, whichever way you choose to approach it. Being open minded to explore, experience, and learn about the different systems of Reiki, I feel, can only help us grow in the experience. Of course, we can have our own preference for a particular Reiki system, just as we can to a

style of teaching and indeed a teacher, but the essence of learning I believe is to expand our awareness and knowledge with insight, variety, and sometimes debate, but more often with inner wisdom.

I want to offer a brief insight into the history of Reiki and just a few of the most common systems of Reiki available; perhaps one or more may resonate with you. This list is by no means conclusive, but my hope is that it may encourage you to further explore an intuitively led path to both the Reiki system and Reiki master who are perfect for you.

In my own teaching I often refer to the fact that I draw on a combination of Japanese-, Eastern-, and Western-type Reiki teachings, but there are actually further classifications.

The classifications include

- Japanese Reiki—often taught in the pure ancient tradition of Mikao Usui's Reiki
- Western Reiki—derived from Hawayo Takata's Reiki
- Tibetan Reiki—traditional Reiki that has strong Tibetan elements such as symbols, influenced, it is thought, by Arthur Robertson
- Eastern Reiki—often includes elements such as chakra and aura healing and may draw on Indian and yogic philosophy, as well as Eastern spiritual practice
- Seichim Reiki—based on concepts of the elements (air, water, earth, fire).
- Traditional and nontraditional Reiki—often based on traditional Usui Reiki but can include crystals, angels, dragons, and elementals, to name but a few.

The many different systems of Reiki that have been developed over the years by various Reiki masters often fall into one or more of these categories. Due to their increase in nature, they have caused some debate as to the legitimacy of each system. As I've already said, I trust that if people truly listen to their inner guidance, they are led to the Reiki system and master who best serves them. I am not here to judge whether one system is better than another, but to offer an honest view of what is available today for anyone looking to learn or experience Reiki.

Generally, we speak in terms of Reiki being around for the past century. I actually believe Reiki is an ancient system that over the centuries has been channeled and delivered in various ways by various cultures, in order for us to connect to our inner knowing of what life is. Globally, there are some truly extraordinary Reiki masters, both present and who have passed, who continue to share the light of Reiki.

Some masters are very prominent in the Reiki world, and some just quietly honor the beauty of Reiki in their own smaller but just as significant way. I don't believe anyone owns Reiki, just as I don't believe anyone owns religion. We are all connected, and it is in community and consolidation that I feel Reiki and the healing of ourselves, each other, and the planet lies. Today, there is of course ownership of trademarks and registrations within the Reiki world. There are also many regulatory organizations that endeavor to uphold professional standards of teaching and delivery. It is my hope that whatever system is taught, it is taught with integrity, authenticity, and commitment.

A brief history of Reiki

Usui Reiki is often referred to as the traditional system of Reiki, and most systems of Reiki today certainly have Usui Reiki at their root.

Mikao Usui (1865–1926), or Usui Sensei as many respectfully refer to him, was thought to be a well-rounded, educated man with an interest in medicine, psychology, and theology. He studied martial arts and traveled extensively before becoming a Buddhist monk. It was at this time (in the early 1920s) that he was guided to undertake a twenty-one-day fast and meditation on Mount Kurama, as part of his spiritual journey. On the twenty-first day of this experience, he received the understanding of Reiki energies as a pathway to self-development, as well as the additional healing aspect of Reiki for self and others. Mount Kurama is consequently considered to be the birthplace of Reiki.

He opened a Reiki clinic in Tokyo and also started a healing society called the Usui Reiki Ryoho Gakkai. Over the next couple of years (especially after the Great Kanto earthquake and tsunami, which brought suffering to thousands of people), he developed his system of Reiki practice, including the Reiki principles or precepts that we know today. It is thought that he taught Reiki to over two thousand people during his lifetime, approximately twenty of whom continued their training to reach the *shinpiden* (master) level.

It is important to note that the story of Mikao Usui and his development of Usui Reiki has changed over the years since I was first attuned. This is not because the original stories were consciously untrue, but that our ability to access more-accurate sources of information about Usui and his attainment and teachings of Reiki has been unveiled. Contrary to early belief, we now know that Mikao Usui was not the first person in Japan to teach Reiki, but that there were actually others teaching Reiki at the time. However, this does not detract from the fundamental impact that Usui Sensei has had on Reiki today.

Two other names that are prominent within the Usui story are that of Chujiro Hayashi (1879–1940) and Hawayo Takata. Hayashi was a retired surgeon from the Japanese navy and a member of the Usui Reiki Ryoho Gakkai. It is thought he was the last master taught by Usui before his death, and that he had been encouraged by Usui Sensei to continue to develop the Reiki system. Hayashi set up a Reiki clinic in Tokyo and developed a system of hand placements that were compiled into a book called the *Hayashi Healing Guide*.

Hawayo Takata was a patient at Hayashi's Reiki clinic. It is said that she was so impressed by the healing she received that she asked Hayashi to teach her Reiki, which he agreed to. It was Takata who later brought Reiki to the West. Takata made many changes and additions to the original system in order for Westerners to accept Reiki. She used to charge $10,000 for an attunement, since she believed this would demand from her students the respect that Reiki deserved. She taught twenty-two students up to master level, many of whom are prominent in our lineages today. Many of them also went on to develop systems of their own.

More and more research is being carried out about the history of Reiki. Hiroshi Doi Sensei, a former member of the Gakkai, has shared much that perhaps would have been kept secret within the Japanese organization. This in turn has helped us develop more of a sense of the original teachings and where the changes have occurred over the years and by whom. However, I encourage my students not to get too caught up in the story of Reiki, but rather to experience what Reiki is for them today. Of course, we greatly honor our lineage and Usui Sensei, but like any tradition or story that has been passed on from master to student, there is often scope and possibility of unconscious change by interpretation.

What is a lineage?

Simply put, a lineage is very much like a family tree. Our lineage tells us our history back to the founder of the system, teacher by teacher. Therefore, for most people who have learned a form of Usui Reiki, their lineage will lead back to Mikao Usui (usually via the Western Reiki route that includes Takata Sensei).

Of course, other systems of Reiki may have begun by a channeling from another master(s) and consequently may have their own lineage. Lineage, like many other aspects of Reiki, continues to be a subject of discussion among the Reiki community.

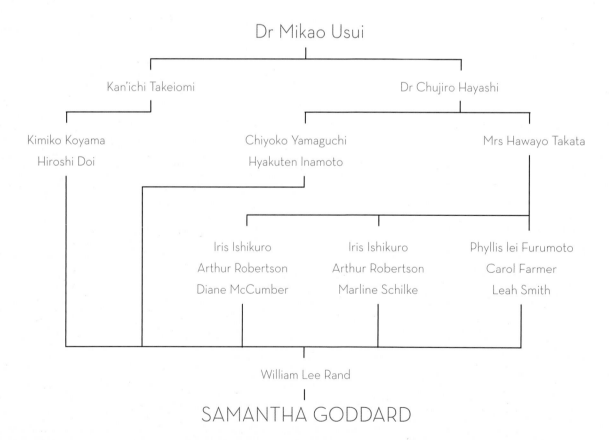

Reiki systems

Here are just a few of the Reiki systems out of the many that have been channeled and developed since the early 1900s. No doubt there will be more. Because our guidance comes from within, I suggest you explore and research the system you are particularly drawn to.

Usui Reiki

This is the first modern form of Reiki that was discovered (or some would say rediscovered) by Dr. Mikao Usui in the early 1900s. Usui Reiki is at the foundation of many other systems that have developed over the years, and is honored as the traditional system.

Usui Shiki Ryoho

Usui Shiki Ryoho was defined by the former lineage bearer Phyllis Lei Furumoto as having four aspects: healing practice, personal development, spiritual discipline, and mystic order, as well as nine elements. It is known as the Usui System of Natural Healing and honors the spiritual lineage of Mikao Usui, Chujiro Hayashi, Hawayo Takata, and Phyllis Lei Furumoto.

Usui/Tibetan Reiki

A Western style of Usui Reiki, influenced by Arthur Robertson (one of Takata's twenty-two masters) and further developed by William Rand. It includes a strong essence of Tibetan Shamanism, including symbols and techniques fused with Usui Shiki Ryoho and traditional techniques.

Jikiden Reiki

Jikiden means to hand down directly without translation, which implies that Jikiden Reiki remains unchanged and pure. It is thought that people who practice Jikiden Reiki pass down a technique that is very similar, if not identical, to Usui Reiki. Frank Ajarva Petter, a prominent Reiki master and international bestselling author of *Reiki Fire, Reiki, the Legacy of Dr. Usui*, and *The Original Reiki Handbook of Dr. Mikao Usui*, to name a few, now teaches Jikiden Reiki in Japan. It is steeped in tradition and has a lineage to Chujiro Hayashi.

Karuna Reiki®

Karuna is a Sanskrit word and is used in Hinduism, Buddhism, and Zen. It is translated to mean any action that is taken to diminish the suffering of others, and could also be translated as compassionate action. It is a system channeled by William Rand. The system includes many symbols and meditations that assist the student to work more closely with all enlightened beings.

Usui / Holy Fire Reiki®

Usui / Holy Fire Reiki® is said to be an evolution of the Usui system and explores a refined healing energy that is continually evolving and contains higher levels of consciousness. William Rand originally received guidance and information about Holy Fire Reiki® during a session with a spiritual advisor in 2014. The term "holy" refers to wholeness and is not religious in nature.

Rainbow Reiki®

This system was developed by Walter Lübeck and is based on the traditional Usui Reiki. It involves extensive research of the origin and roots of Reiki, Reiki symbols, mantras, meditation, and spiritual psychology. It also involves several unique techniques such as astral traveling, karma clearing, and crystal healing. The intention is to strengthen relations to spirits such as deities and angels that help in the expansion of healing possibilities and personal development.

Kundalini Reiki

This system was developed by Danish Reiki master Ole Gabrielsen. It is a form of Reiki that emphasizes the acceleration of personal development by awakening the Kundali energy within. Kundalini is Sanskrit for "snake" or "serpent" power and is referred to as the energy of consciousness that rises through the body, inviting transformation.

Symbols in Reiki

Symbols can be found in many of the Reiki systems. The accuracy of when they were introduced in the Usui lineage and by whom has changed. However, for many they remain an important and beautiful part of Reiki practice.

Reiki symbols are sacred in their nature. Although it is now possible to search their history, design, and meaning on the internet, my feeling is that they have no real meaning unless a student has been through Reiki training. During training, the symbols are passed on to the student during a specific ceremony, and it is only then that the symbols come alive or are activated.

Symbols allow us to have a certain focus on the Reiki energy for a specific purpose. A student of mine once referred to them as a useful hook into a chosen vibration and intention. Many of the Reiki symbols are derived from Japanese Kanji. Traditionally there are four main symbols in Usui Reiki, but in other systems there may be many more.

My guidance is to not reveal too much information about the Reiki symbols in this book. I feel strongly about the right of passage for individuals to embrace the Reiki symbols: their pathway and their gifts. I also feel it would potentially lessen part of the magic in their discovery through traditional channels. What I will say is that in my experience, each symbol carries a distinctive vibration, and that their use ranges from grounding to balance to opening the gateway to distance healing.

RIDING LIFE'S WAVES

Riding life's waves

I often like to reference the analogy of surfing when I'm teaching Reiki. I explain how I have had times in my life where I feel I have caught that perfect wave and am literally riding life: everything seems to flow naturally and has an ease and grace to it that is not only nourishing but also life-affirming. Some of those waves truly bring the most peaceful of rides, feeling totally at one with the water, the board, and the elements. Other rides can be exhilarating, others totally terrifying. Whatever the ride, there is always one thing that is certain— that all waves end. We inevitably, at some point, will fall off our board and back into the sea. This is how we surf life: for days, months, even years, it can all be going so well, and then, inevitably through various circumstances, chance, or beliefs, we fall off our boards.

The invitation on this often-ungraceful departure from our board is not to beat ourselves up but to understand that it is a natural and very significant part of our journey. Perhaps it is simply time to pause from the constant striving. Sometimes it takes years to wait for the right wave to feel safe enough to jump back on our boards, occasionally only a matter of minutes. Sometimes life can feel like we are literally cut off from our board and we can see it floating away in the distance. Yet, if we can, it's important to allow ourselves to accept this fall as a natural part of the process.

In addition, I know myself that in some of the hardest times of my life, I seemingly have resisted easy access to returning to my board and the flow of life. This was not a particularly conscious decision or because my support board had left me, but because there was some old energetic pattern being played out. Usually something around a belief of not being worthy that was stopping me getting back on. This is just one common belief that many of us may find in our pot. An old belief system that may have been started in childhood, or perhaps from a parent, teacher, ex-partner, boss, or colleague. Often these kinds of beliefs can come into our lives on a very subtle energetic level; other times, they can be harshly and firmly installed. Whatever their origin,

their ability to form strong neural pathways often knock us from our conscious knowing of choice, to slipping back into a well-trodden but not always useful pathway of behavior. It is these energetic pathways of behavior and beliefs that Reiki can help us heal in order for clarity of choice and inner knowing to return. It is an opportunity for us to ask the question "Does this belief or behavior serve me?" and to understand that its subsequent block created in our lives, body, and mind is energetic.

By connecting with Reiki energy and our truth, we can become empowered in the knowledge that we can shift and change. We are able to release this lower vibrational belief, heal the blockage, and ultimately attract patterns of higher vibration into our lives. We embark on a journey of growth from what is referred to as our culturally created self, and with commitment begin to unveil and become our authentic self.

Nothing is more precious than being in the present moment. Fully alive, fully aware.

—Thich Nhat Hanh

The point to remember is that falling off our board is okay, as is having these unhelpful beliefs. It is normal; we are human. Most of us have lives that include work, family, children, everyday stress, and influence: as much as we may dream of spiritual retreat in faraway places of beauty, solitude, and prayer, we generally find ourselves in the real world. Yet for me, that fact is a significant part of this story and raises the question "How do we integrate into our daily lives that which in those moments of flow we recognize as true and present living?"

This is the gift of Reiki: the practice of presence and energetic awareness to create flow in a world that can so easily be debilitating. I have found Reiki to be a true provider of the opportunity to bring, if you like, a little bit of heaven to our earth, our reality.

However, Reiki is not about the quick fix that is so frequently looked for in modern society. It offers us a lifelong journey (and maybe longer, depending on your beliefs). Once we discover a support system, be that Reiki or any other form of spiritual or energetic support, we are literally invited in for the long haul. I am aware that for some this can be a daunting prospect and too overwhelming to comprehend. But there's no rush. One step at a time: one moment at a time. One of the beautiful aspects of learning Reiki is that it will never leave you. It is said that once you have had an attunement to Reiki that your ability to channel Reiki energy will always be with you. There is of course a pathway, which looks different for each of us. Yet, it is in learning to be present and accessing our truth that our journey often begins.

Being present:
an exercise to "check in"

This is a very simple invitation to explore how you are at any given moment. It is an easy exercise that can be done at work, at home, in fact wherever you can honor yourself with a few minutes of quiet time.

Simply sit with your feet on the ground and gently allow your focus to rest on the natural in-and-out flow of your breath. Follow your breath for a few moments and then, when you feel comfortable, allow the breath to become a little deeper, breathing down into your belly space. This area is often referred to as our area of knowing. When you can feel your breath in your belly, allow your focus to also rest down in this space deep inside your body, and really connect with your physical self in this moment.

Learning to really listen to your body can be an incredibly enlightening experience, since our body will often tell us all of the information that we need to know. If you think about it, how often do we override our body's response to something? If we truly listen to our body, we can start to return to our truth.

So, with your focus gently resting on the breath and the connection of your physical body, now quietly ask yourself the question "How am I? How am I right now in this moment?" and honor yourself by listening.

Notice any potential resistance to what may arise as you listen. It may be a color that you notice, a thought, a feeling—but often our ego may wish to change or override our body's response. However, if we can start to really listen and learn to bring through our deep knowing, it begins to change the root of the answer from auto-response to truth.

Strength comes from living your truth. To be true and authentic is your path to happiness, peace, and joy.

—*Anonymous*

土
ground

FINDING YOUR GROUND

Finding your ground

I believe that grounding is one of the essential elements of energetic work and, in fact, life. For those who know me, they will often refer (with a smile or in some cases a slight grimace) to my persistent invitation of learning to ground. That's because I believe it is a fundamental tool to ensure our sustainability in whatever pathway we choose in life.

Of course, I imagine my invitation to others to become aware of their own grounding is a direct result of having had to learn to ground myself in order to maintain balance and clarity in my own life.

Similarly, I continually see in my private clinic work that 99 percent of the clients who come to me—whatever the physical, emotional, or spiritual reason—will inevitably have lost their grounding. When we experience times of challenge, it is often the case that our grounding has been compromised. Therefore, learning to ground ourselves is incredibly important since it ensures healthy awareness of our needs—and that is where our work begins.

Grounding is one of the most important lessons we learn through Reiki. Without grounding, very little in life is sustainable. The invitation is to learn what it is that makes us ungrounded, and to know our triggers. Only then can we choose to check in, take a breath, and arrive into the present moment. In this way, we are able to move away from a reactive state to one of solidity: our ground, our core, and our knowing.

Grounding can mean different things to different people, but I feel it is essentially our connection to (Mother) Earth—a connection that can literally help us feel stable, strong, and steady. Consequently, this leads to our connection to our body—our sense of embodiment. As with many of the tools we learn, the way to know if we are grounded is to recognize the signs of being ungrounded.

Common words and feelings associated with each:

GROUNDED	UNGROUNDED
Clarity	Cloudy
Safe	Unsafe
Present	Lost
Secure	Insecure
Embodied	Heady
Home	All over the place
Connected	Disconnected
Solid	Wobbly
Calm	Triggered

Grounding is what I call a lifetime lesson. It is not something that we necessarily master and never have to worry about again. In fact, it is something that I encourage students to embrace as a habitual opportunity. It is important to remember that the more you practice grounding, the easier it can become. It is a skill, like any other, that needs cultivating and care. It has become the first question I ask myself when I'm having a bad day: "Am I grounded?"

There are many ways to ground oneself, which include

- Grounding exercises, meditations, and visualization
- Present-moment living
- Mindful walking
- Grounding food
- Cultivating one's connection to nature
- Gardening
- Forest bathing
- Connecting to or hugging a tree
- Grounding crystals
- Healing the root chakra
- Elements of yoga
- Running

I know that if I am feeling ungrounded, I am often drawn to visit the sea. Other times, it will be a walk in the woods or a trek in the mountains. Sometimes simply going out in nature and seeing what you are drawn to can help you reconnect with the Earth. I have often found that picking up a shell, flower, conker, or leaf can be just as grounding and insightful as working with a crystal.

I have had students say their home is their grounding place—although of course for some, home may be the cause of their ungrounding. It really is up to the individual to work out the best grounding tools and spaces for himself or herself and to appreciate that sometimes these may change.

In class, I often share the "growing your roots" or "dropping your anchor" meditation for students to get a sense of what it feels like in their body to be grounded. Generally, the words used to describe the feeling after one of these meditations is heavy, rooted, or solid; in addition, having a sense of weight in their legs and feet. I refer to this as "having your Reiki boots on."

Exercise 3

Dropping-the-anchor meditation

The intention of this meditation is for you to feel connected to the ground with a solid awareness of your root and feet, so you feel embodied and therefore your energies are fully present. It is a useful meditation since it can be practiced fairly quickly and discreetly; therefore, it is often one that I share for using at work.

1. Begin by finding a comfortable sitting position with your back upright and your feet planted on the floor.

2. Gently allow your awareness to rest on your breath, and begin to observe your natural in-and-out flow of breath, as always without judgment or the need to change it, but just to come into a place of noticing.

3. When you are ready, engage the soles of your feet by visualizing that you are breathing in through the soles of your feet, allowing the breath to travel equally up through both legs, rising up the midline of your body, and out through your crown. For the exhalation, visualize the breath coming down through your body and traveling out again through the soles of your feet.

4. Continue with this breathing and allow yourself to really feel the connection at these two points of contact with the ground—your feet.

5. As and when you feel ready, and on your next exhalation, visualize that you "drop your 'energetic' anchor" down through the crown of your head. Let it drop down your midline and leave the body through your root chakra, to firmly connect with the ground.

6. With the next inhalation, the invitation is to breathe in through these three points of contact with the floor (the soles of your feet and your anchor), for the breath to "meet" at your root, and for it to then continue its journey up the midline of your body and out of the crown. On the exhalation, the breath leaves the body again through the three points of contact with the ground.

7. Continue this for as long as you feel guided. When you are ready, allow yourself to drop the visualization and allow the breath to gently return to its natural rhythm.

8. Take note of how your body feels.

Grounding crystals

In terms of grounding, you may wish to explore the following crystals as a potential basic grounding set to work with

Black tourmaline
Hematite (Rainbow hematite illustrated)
Jasper
Smoky quartz
Tiger's eye

It can be helpful to research when working with crystals, but equally helpful to listen to your internal guide as to what your body and energies need. This may be by using a pendulum or simply seeing what crystal you are drawn to. There are obviously some fabulous books and teachers offering advice in regard to what crystal is best used for a specific purpose; however, my own experience is that not one size fits all.

There is much to learn about crystals and the safe, effective ways of using them. As small and pretty as they can often be, I would invite you to never underestimate their potential potency. I have had quite extensive training with crystals, yet I would admit to only really having just scraped the surface. They can be a wonderful addition to Reiki practice or a powerful force of their own, and certainly one that is well worth exploring, should you have the calling.

Crystal healing

This exercise provides a simple and effective crystal-healing layout for grounding and centering. You will need:

A space to lie down
The phone off
Two smoky quartz crystals

This simple layout is intended to help bring a sense of grounding to your mind and body, particularly if you are feeling overwhelmed, scattered, or confused.

As always, you will need to have cleansed your crystals to begin with.

To do this, set your intention for the crystals to be cleansed and then place them in the sunlight or moonlight for a few hours; rinse them in fresh spring water or use sound or sacred smoke to assist in this process. For ease, I often place my crystals in a singing bowl and strike it to allow the vibration of the sound to cleanse the crystal. With practice you can often hear the sound purify with each strike as the crystal is cleansed.

Lie down in a comfortable position and place one smoky quartz at the base of your throat and the other between your legs.

Stay there for as long as you are guided, setting your intention for the crystals to provide grounding and focus on your physical reality.

INTENTION IS A POWERFUL THING

Intention is a powerful thing

In dictionary terms, an intention is an idea that you plan (or intend) to carry out. If you mean something, it's an intention. Your goal, purpose, or aim is your intention. It's something you mean to do, whether you pull it off or not.

Before taking this path, I didn't appreciate how such a small, and what can be thought of as insignificant, word could have such an impact on our lives on so many levels. When anyone asks me, "So how does Reiki work?," quite simply I could reply that it is driven by our intention. Most of us have no idea just how powerful a being we are and how our intentions in life can mean the difference between pain and happiness, connection and disconnection, and so much more.

Intention in Reiki is, I believe, the element of empowerment within the process. It is our wish to be a clear channel, and to work with the highest vibrational energies available to us for our highest good, as well as that of others. It is working with energetic intention that clears the spirit of lower vibrational energy. Or, to put it another way, the parts of our ego that are potentially unevolved, in order to achieve Source connection and ultimately the healing we seek.

On so many occasions, I have taught a Reiki class stating that what I was about to share with the students was not rocket science, but something that on some level we already know how to do. However, it is not until we reach the part about intention that this question arises: "Really, it's that simple?" Yes, in some ways it is. We intend Reiki to flow and it flows; we intend to

channel love and light of the highest vibrational potency and so we learn to channel. Our energetic intention and thought is one of the most powerful tools we have, yet most of us don't really appreciate how to use it.

It is important to state here that in no way am I belittling or negating the time, courage, dedication, commitment, honoring, and surrender that is called upon on this path of self-mastery. Just because something is simple, it most certainly does not make it easy. Yet, our intention is something that we can form and grow a true relationship with. If we truly believe that we have a part to play in our present moment, then we can be empowered in the knowledge that the beautiful tool of Reiki is accessible to all.

Be careful what you wish for, lest it come true! For me, this phrase is a reminder of how powerful our thoughts can be, and therefore their outcomes. It comes from *Aesop's Fables*, one of the best-known collections of morality tales, dating from around 260 BCE.

Once we start to recognize that our thoughts and intentions are vibrational in nature, then life begins to take a different perspective. Particularly when we understand how each vibrational pattern summons a similar vibrational pattern into our lives.

Celebrated books such as *The Secret*, *The Power of Thought*, and *Law of Attraction* all delve into the incredible power of thought, and how we can therefore have influence over our own lives and what we attract into it, from both a positive and negative perspective.

Affirmations

Affirmations are positive statements that we can adopt in order to translate our clear intention into a positive verbal format and finally into a manifestation. By understanding that our thoughts and, in addition, our words are energetic and therefore ultimately impact our universal energetic existence, we can learn to choose our thoughts and words carefully and with precision, so we are able to cultivate a positive language.

Clarity in Reiki is essential in determining our clear connection to Source energy and nothing else. If we are essentially choosing to channel energy that is universal, we want to ensure that it is always of the highest and purest nature.

As I referred to earlier, just because Reiki in one glance may appear simple, it is far from it. In my experience, this is a discipline that takes practice, but the results can be remarkable, as is developing the skill of affirmation and manifestation.

Louise Hay was known as the Queen of Affirmation, and her book *Heal Your Body: The Mental Causes for Physical Illness and the Metaphysical Way to Overcome Them* was an introduction for many people around the world to the type of language we can use in working with affirmations directly linked with physical ailments. She explains her revelations on discovering the concept of metaphysical causations, which describes the power in the words and thoughts that create experiences.

Her approach in the book details the problem, probable cause, and new thought pattern and offers an alternative insight into underlying energetic attachment to existing physical scenarios.

For example

Problem: nausea

Probable cause: fear. Rejecting an idea or experience.

New thought pattern: I am safe. I trust the process of life to bring only good to me.

Although there are hundreds of very helpful suggested affirmations, it is also incredibly empowering to write your own. It's a wonderful opportunity to connect to your truth at any given time and introduce to your life what it is that you need in the present moment, be that physically, emotionally, or spiritually.

Generally, affirmations start with "I am . . . ," ensuring they are stated in the present as a given, rather than a wish for the future. These often-simple phrases, used in conjunction with Reiki, can be a potent combination but are also a beautiful daily and empowering practice on their own.

Exercise 5

Creating a personal affirmation

There are different ways of creating and practicing positive affirmations, from simply writing them down on a piece of paper to actively saying them to yourself in front of a mirror.

As mentioned, the affirmation is a simple statement, usually beginning with "I am," but always in the present tense. This helps us reshape our beliefs and move toward manifesting life goals, positive beliefs, and behavior.

To do this, you will need a quiet space, a pen, paper, and the phone switched off.

1. Sit comfortably, either on the floor or at a table, with your pen and paper at hand.

2. Close your eyes and take a moment to connect to your breath.

3. When you feel your mind and body starting to settle, bring to mind a habit that may not serve you, or something that you would like to change about yourself. I would encourage you to start with something simple: for example, the habit may be simply being late too often.

4. Once you have an idea, open your eyes and write it down on the piece of paper.

5. Then gently allow yourself to close your eyes once more and reconnect with your breath and invite yourself to find a counterstatement to the one you have just written on the piece of paper. For example, "I am honoring my time and that of others."

6. Once again, open your eyes and now write this down underneath your original statement.

7. Say it out loud to yourself and see if the words resonate; if so, this or a simplified version can become your affirmation.

8. One of the key aspects of affirmation is repetition. It is important that you repeat your affirmation on a daily basis in order to really establish the energetic connection to the statement, as well as the subsequent neural pathway that is being created in your mind.

9. Visual affirmations can also be really powerful, and these could include

- Writing your affirmation on a sticky note and placing it in a prominent position where you are likely to see it on a regular basis
- Setting a daily reminder on your phone in the form of an alarm to prompt you to repeat your affirmation
- Writing regular affirmations in a journal

Just for today, I will let go of anger.

Just for today, I will let go of worry.

Just for today, I will be humble.

Just for today, I will be honest.

Just for today, I will be kind to myself,
as well as others.

The Reiki precepts

The Reiki precepts or ideals are a set of intentions that lie at the heart of many Reiki systems. They have been passed down through the majority of Reiki lineages from master to student, as an original offering from Dr Mikao Usui. A precept is a code of practice, and it is said that Usui taught them to his students to support them on their spiritual journey and self-healing path. I see them as a set of intentions that underline the complete system of Reiki and offer a grounding for students (which we all are) to follow on a daily basis.

Many years ago, when I first started Reiki I learned the precepts in simplified form, which is how they are often referenced, but I have also included their longer, original voice. Although simple in their nature, to live by these precepts can be much harder than we first imagine.

For me, what makes them accessible for most of us is the invitation of "just for today." Yes, the language may be simple, but actually to truly and authentically live by these intentions can be a relentless and often-challenging path. However, I know for myself that if I am asked to try to abide by a certain invitation, then I would hope a day may be achievable, but the thought of a lifetime may be a different matter. One day at a time . . .

The original Reiki ideals:

The secret art of inviting happiness.

The miraculous medicine of all diseases.

Just for today, do not be angry.

Do not worry and be filled with gratitude.

Devote yourself to your work and be kind to people.

Every morning and evening, join your hands in prayer.

Pray these words to your heart.

And chant these words with your mouth.

—The founder, Mikao Usui

Other tools of manifestation

A dream board, also called a vision board, is a beautiful way of visually representing aims, goals, dreams, and intentions.

Creating a dream board / vision board enables us to identify with our intentions and dreams in a physical way, while also engaging with our own creative energy. Dream boards can be made from anything you wish, including natural objects, photos, drawings, magazine clippings, or even poetry. It is important that they are unique and relay anything that may inspire or motivate you on your journey.

The board is usually best placed somewhere like your bedroom or office, where you can easily add, remove, change, or incorporate anything you are guided to include on a regular basis. The invitation is to have fun with it and allow it to be a free-moving piece of you and your dreams.

Crystals can also be wonderful to explore in relation to manifestation. A good crystal to start with is clear quartz, since it is known to amplify our energetic vibration and hold intention. Crystals are often used in conjunction with Reiki but can be beautiful energetic tools in themselves.

Some believe that a candle's flame is a metaphor for the soul, and that by burning and meditating with a candle, we can strengthen our purpose as we sit with the flame in unison and watch it burn with the desire of our intention.

Similarly, music is thought of as a metaphor for our spirit. Over the centuries, music has been an integral part of ceremony and celebration. For many of us, it acts as an incredible supportive energy as well as connects us to our tribal ancestry. By immersing ourselves in music, we can become one with its vibration and intent.

Color can have a huge impact on our mood, general well-being, and connection. We may notice that we are drawn to wear a particular color or bring a particular color into our home. This is because color also has a vibration that is absorbed into our nervous system and therefore can support a positive outlook and intention.

As a simple manifestation tool, writing a journal can help us safely express and explore our beliefs by bringing a voice to our feelings. It can help us define our intentions and purpose and incorporate both the practice of affirmations and gratitude.

The greatest achievement was at first and for a time a dream. The oak sleeps in the acorn, the bird waits in the egg, and in the highest vision of the soul a waking angel stirs. Dreams are the seedlings of realities.

—James Allen (nineteenth-century English writer)

DROP THE MONKEYS

Drop the monkeys

In order to embark on an authentic healing path, we must first determine what is ours to heal. We have to learn to be discerning.

What I mean by this statement is that as energetic beings we are capable of (and in some cases very good at) absorbing other people's energies, often to the detriment of our self. Although this may happen unconsciously, it can lead to becoming completely energetically overwhelmed and provide huge challenges for people who find themselves absorbing too much. A label often ascribed to people with this spongelike quality is of being highly sensitive, or more properly, an empath, of which I know hundreds—myself included.

I remember teaching a Reiki class once and explaining this concept when one of the students burst into tears. When I asked if she was okay, she replied, "You have just explained to me in one sentence, something that has affected me my whole life." Sometimes just knowing that there is a name to use, accept, and manage this overwhelming feeling is enough to shift it from being a burden to a gift that we can work with.

Like any sensitivity, I like to refer to it as a gift, since there can be hidden magic underneath the normally rocky road of managing such behavior. By learning tools to form strong energetic boundaries and really listening to our intuition, we can not only learn from what our body is telling us, but also use this to empower our sense of choice in life. Of course, one such tool is Reiki.

My son, Arthur, has always been able to determine whether somewhere is safe or not for him to enter. When I say safe, I mean energetically, since it is not only people who carry energy and vibration but buildings as well. As a child it is generally accepted that a point-blank refusal to enter somewhere can be put down to the child having a moment. But in my world, I understand it to be far more than that. I believe it's a child's own energetic alarm system as to what may or may not serve to be safe to them. Arthur may not consciously understand why he feels unsafe to enter a certain room or building, but on some level it will be an energetic awareness to a lower vibration that he is not willing to be part of.

Obviously, as adults, we can't throw a tantrum outside a building; instead we tend to override our intuitive sense and just walk in. This is of course fine with energetic awareness and strong boundaries in place, but it can get a little more troublesome without.

Another example of a time that you may have felt this sense of hesitation is when you enter a house where perhaps the couple who invited you for dinner has just had a row. They of course may act as if everything is fine as they welcome their guests. Yet, even without verbal acknowledgment of the disagreement, you can feel the argument still in the air. If you are sensitive to energy, it is very easy to absorb this potential lower vibrational energy and carry it around with you for the rest of the evening. The same is true of any energetic exchange; if we are not mindful, then potentially we will take on and literally carry the energy of those exchanges throughout our day.

Now consider that energetic exchange is constant in our lives: from the moment we wake up in the morning until the moment we sleep (and that's not even starting on the subject of dreams). From a crowded subway car, to a hectic supermarket, to a heated email exchange, phone call, or text, it is endless. You can therefore imagine that over time, lower vibrational energy can become extremely heavy and exhausting. In my experience, it can subsequently be the route of many physical and mental health issues.

In addition to daily encounters, there is also the belief that we carry energetic patterning from our parents, DNA, ancestral line, and even past lives. All of these ideas, whatever your belief system, can start to have some resonance when we become more aware of our own energetic patterns and those of the people around us. Within the scientific community, people are also researching and recognizing that the physical body, as well as our energetic bodies, carries energy from our past. This is referred to as cell memory and is a fascinating subject to explore.

Monkeys

It is not a coincidence that many people who are called to learn Reiki may consider themselves fixers or fall into a category of wanting to help others. In some cases, not only is this a calling of compassion and service, but it is important to recognize that it may also be because a familiar energetic pattern exists—perhaps a pattern of helping others that may, on a deeper level, be a desire to take away their pain. This is often derived from early learning, or ever prior lifetime experience. Sometimes it becomes not even a choice of wanting to help others, but a conditioning of our energetic self to absorb the energies around us.

Back in my corporate days, I remember reading a book called *The One Minute Manager* by Ken Blanchard and Spencer Johnson, which referenced an act of carrying monkeys. In corporate terms, this was an analogy to describe the need for delegation. It told you to recognize if you were indeed a person who was happy to take on everyone else's monkeys, even to the detriment of yourself. I now understand that those monkeys are energy.

The act of cleansing

There are three golden invitations that I like to share during my Reiki I (first level) class. They are to cleanse, protect, and, as you know, ground. These acts, intentions, and practices serve as a way of preparing oneself before any kind of healing or energy work, be that on ourselves or on others. For me, they are the foundations of our healing path and fundamental tools to ensure wellness in all aspects of our being—not to mention incredibly positive habits to adopt in everyday life.

The act of energetic cleansing can enable us to free our self, others, or a space of vibration that may be low in energy, so not serving us and, importantly, not ours to carry in the first place. Protection can ensure we remain within our own cleansed energy by forming strong energetic boundaries through intention, visualization, or even crystals.

Kenyoku (which literally translates as dry bathing) is a Japanese Reiki technique that can be a very effective tool of cleansing. I teach *Kenyoku* in my Reiki I classes but also share it with many of my clients as an effective tool to use at work, in the home, or as a daily practice.

Again, it is driven by intention and a strong sense of purpose, but I have witnessed many people surprised by how effective such a simple technique can be.

Exercise 6

How to practice Kenyoku

1. Bring your hands into gasshô position (which is where your hands are together, palms touching, in front of your heart), then set your intention for the practice.

2. Place your right hand on your left shoulder.

3. Inhale and, as you strongly exhale, brush your hand from your shoulder, down across the body, and off the right hip.

4. Repeat this on the other side.

5. Repeat again on the original side.

6. Extend your left arm.

7. Place your right hand on your left shoulder.

8. Inhale and, as you strongly exhale, brush your hand along the length of your extended arm and off the fingertips of your left hand. Let your hand continue into the air as if sweeping off any negative energy. As you do so, visualize any negative energy transforming into golden sparkles and being lifted back to Source. Alternatively, some people like to visualize it being absorbed and recycled by the Earth.

9. Repeat on the other side, using the extended right arm.

10. Repeat on the original side.

11. Bring your hands back to gasshô position, inviting a sense of gratitude for this ritual and your cleansed body and aura.

The ancient ritual of smudging

One of the most ancient ways to energetically cleanse is the ceremony of smudging. This ritual entails the burning of a sacred plant (usually white sage) and evoking the smoke and spirit of the plant to assist in releasing any negative or low vibrational energy. In addition, clear intention or prayer is used to send the energy back to Source or, in some variations, to Mother Earth for renewal. Native American and other indigenous cultures have used herbs and plants for such ceremonies and intentions for centuries. It can be a truly uplifting ritual, as well as a very useful everyday tool to clear any unwanted energy from yourself, others, or your home.

Choosing your tools

First, choose the plant that you wish to burn during your ceremony. A few that you may consider are:

Cedar—to help clear negative emotions and therefore purify

Lavender—to restore balance and calm energy

Sage—traditionally used to purify people and places before a sacred ceremony

There are of course many other aromatics you can choose from. However, it is important, when using any kind of plant or herb, to honor and respect the healing power and potency they uphold, and to ensure there is no potential for allergic reaction.

The traditional shamanic method of smudging uses a shell to house and burn the plant/herb, and a feather to fan the smoke. However, an alternative and just-as-effective method is to use a smudge stick, which is basically a wand made of the leaves of one or more of the plants, tied together and dried. This in itself can be something beautiful to make but can also be bought.

In addition, you will need
- a fireproof bowl (or shell) to hold underneath the smudge stick while it burns to catch any ashes or embers
- matches to light the candle
- a candle to light the smudge stick
- a bowl of sand to properly extinguish the smudge stick after the ceremony is complete
- Tibetan chimes (not essential, but lovely to include if you have some) to end the ceremony with vibrational sound

How to smudge your home

Before you begin the ceremony, ensure that you feel grounded and that you have enough space and time to do so without interruption. Smudging can take as little or as long as you wish, but being prepared and mindful is essential. This ceremony can be done on your own or with your family. Contemplate what it is that you wish to invite into your home once the space is cleared. As always, intention is key. The following is a guideline of how to smudge your home, but I invite you to listen to your own guidance as to what feels right. You'll know intuitively in what

areas to linger, in what direction to walk, in what space you will need to repeat your intention. Trust what comes to you when you are in the process.

It is usually a good idea to start at the entrance door and move in a clockwise direction around your home, but again, feel into your guidance. You simply need to light the smudge stick so that it produces smoke but is not burning heavily, since it is the smoke that you will use during the ceremony.

Waft the smudge stick with intention as you walk around the rooms, ensuring the smoke reaches into the areas that call you, and as you do so, state your intention of wishing to clear your home of any energies that do not serve you or your family and to ensure the space is cleansed to accept love, protection, and pure vibrational energy into your home, for your highest good.

Some people use a simple prayer or mantra that may resonate, such as the Tibetan Buddhist mantra *Om mani padme hum*, which is the mantra of compassion. I often use my Reiki symbols, which invite pure vibrational energy into the space. Use whatever feels right for you, as long as it has clarity.

Move around your home, including the staircase and any floors you have, and finish back at the front door with a final statement of intent. You could even visualize your home filled with a golden light and surrounded by a protected field of energy.

To finish, ensure that your smudge stick has been properly extinguished in the bowl of sand, and invite a sense of gratitude for your beautifully cleansed home.

As you can imagine, this is a wonderful ritual to perform when you first move into a new home, but it can be used as often as you wish. As well as smudging your home, you can also smudge yourself, others, objects, crystals, and spaces.

RED PILL, BLUE PILL?

Red pill, blue pill?

A common thread that I see so often in my work is the fact that clients have lost sight of the fact that they have choices in life. Of course, that is not something that is just consistent with my clients, but a trait I recognize from periods of my own life, as well as many people whom I have met over the years.

It's that oppressive and often-overwhelming feeling of being stuck.

Maybe it's stuck in a job, a house, a relationship, or a seemingly never-ending pattern of behavior, as we touched on earlier. Wherever the feeling originates from, it can be one that weighs incredibly heavy on our mind and soul and inevitably can turn down our light and sense of who we are. It can push us into a corner of self-doubt and ultimately slowly eat away at our ability to have a voice or be able to change our situation.

It can be very easy for society to dictate our pathway, with the incessant noise and demands that are placed on us. Not to mention, the additional sense of expectation from our parents, partners, friends, colleagues, and even countless strangers that we may gather via various social media platforms. It is easy to get lost in the noise instead of listening to our inner knowing. We can unwittingly become finely tuned to hearing only the "shoulds" that surround us. You *should* do this job, you *should* wear this outfit, you *should* meet this person, you *should* behave a certain way.

Personally, the word "should" has become one of my most vibrant warning flags. It indicates to me that I am potentially out of my power and listening to a voice that may not be in line with my inner truth. Reiki has been instrumental in helping me become aware of this happening; in fact, Reiki has been instrumental to helping me become aware . . . full stop.

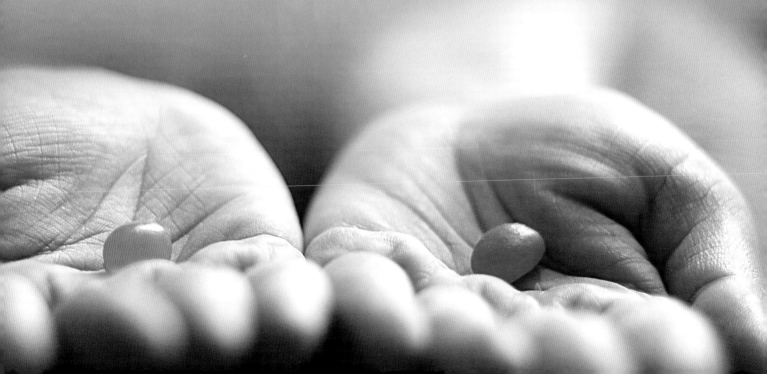

Awareness is all about

restoring your freedom

to choose what you want,

instead of what your past

imposes on you.

—Deepak Chopra

Often when I meet potential Reiki students or clients, they are at a crossroads. They may initially use the self-description of being stuck or blocked. However, on reflection, a deeper sense of self has guided them to seek assistance, since they undoubtedly feel something isn't right. This usually presents a crossroads.

I go on to explain that it can be a call to awaken by embarking on a journey with Reiki; that is, to awaken from the life choices that may be keeping them asleep and stuck in their current cycle. A cinematic example of this is when Neo in the movie *The Matrix* is offered two pills by Morpheus—a blue pill or a red pill. One will ensure that Neo stays in his current state of denial to the truth and continue living in a false world, and the other pill will show him the stark reality of life and its challenges but will ultimately set him free.

Drawing on this comparison may be a little dramatic, I grant you. Yet, for me, the analogy is not far off the choice we have when we decide to be present and awaken on our energetic and spiritual journey. This choice brings a shift to our perception of ourselves and the world, a world that can offer such diversity, breadth, and beauty in place of potentially a far duller and narrow existence. Of course, it is our choice what we do with our experience of awakening, yet, time and time again, I have seen that once awake, it is very difficult to return to being asleep.

Being awake through presence, energetic awareness, growth, and flow is a path available to us at our crossroads. However, it is available to us not just once, but over and over again. As we continue with our Reiki self-mastery and service to others, so other crossroads appear, with further choices laid out in front of us. It may become easier to hear and see them, but not necessarily easier to take those steps. Change constantly requires courage.

Rituals

To develop courage is to develop an unyielding belief in the worth of your own life and purpose. This can take time and commitment, but to live with courage is to be free. In addition to Reiki practice, a beautiful way to cultivate courage can be through ritual.

Ritual comes in many forms but is often a simple ceremony that is repeated with intent. I have found ritual to be a powerful tool in my toolkit, and I therefore want to share a couple of my favorites with you.

This a courage ritual that I came across many years ago. It can be held with others, but it is equally powerful when held on your own. For thousands of years, ritual has been carried out around the time of a full moon, but choose a time that feels right for you. If possible, it is wonderful to embark on this ritual outside with a fire, but simply having a candle large enough to safely burn a piece of paper is also suitable.

Make a circle with flowers, stones, or whatever feels appropriate to create a sacred space around the candle/fire.

You may wish to begin the ritual with some form of music, whether that is recorded or by playing an instrument to a simple beat. I often use my drum and trust whatever comes through. When you feel connected to the sacred space and your intention, take a piece of paper and write down the fears that may be blocking the pursuit of your true self.

When you have acknowledged what you have written, burn the piece of paper, reciting this blessing:

I accept I have fears

I am not my fears

I am now cleansed and renewed

I go forward with courage at my side

You may wish to bring your hands into prayer position, bowing your head while saying a silent prayer of gratitude.

The second is a simple ritual that can be carried out by a river, lake, or ocean, whenever you are guided.

Pick up a stone in your right hand and walk with it, thinking of what is troubling you. When you are ready, hold it with clarity and say out loud: "All ill be gone," then throw it into the water.

Then pick up a stone with your left hand and say aloud: "All good become." Put it in your pocket and take it home.

Our deepest fear is not that we are inadequate. Our deepest fear is that we are powerful beyond measure. It is our light, not our darkness, that most frightens us. We ask ourselves, "Who am I to be brilliant, gorgeous, talented, fabulous?" Actually, who are we not to be? You are a child of God. Your playing small doesn't serve the world.

There is nothing enlightened about shrinking so that other people won't feel insecure around you. We were born to manifest the glory of God within us. It is not just in some of us, it is in everyone, and as we let our own lights shine, we unconsciously give other people permission to do the same. As we are liberated from our own fear, our presence automatically liberates other.

—*Marianne Williamson*

母
mother

THE JOURNEY OF MOTHERHOOD

The journey of motherhood

As I sit down to write this chapter, I notice that I am acutely aware of taking a deep inhalation as the words "Where do I start?" form a rather dominant thought bubble in front of my eyes. This is not because I feel it is a daunting task, but I am reminded of my passion around this subject and my need to be succinct as to how Reiki can help in this area.

At the age of thirty-eight, I found myself labeled as one of those women who were deemed an old mother and, therefore, potentially high risk. As is often my response to labels, I didn't give it too much thought at the time, since in my mind it was the time in my life when I had chosen to have a baby, so to me it was the right time.

Pregnancy, birth, and all that follows is no doubt a unique experience to every woman (and man). However, my experience of pregnancy and birth led me to become passionate about supporting other women on this incredible journey, equally exquisite in joy and pain. There is still a huge misconception and projection of what pregnancy, birth, and motherhood should be like, which can unconsciously lead a lot of women down a very unexpected rabbit hole of disbelief, judgment, and isolation.

Of course, some women are blessed with a journey of ease through this incredible transition. Yet, whether it is with ease or with challenge, through my own experience I feel it is truly a life-changing time, in which Reiki can play an incredibly supportive role—from conception, through the pregnancy, during birth, and very much beyond.

Conception

Reiki can be a hugely beneficial aid to assist couples in conceiving. It can

- Significantly reduce stress levels and induce a state of deep relaxation to body and mind
- Help bring balance to the physical, emotional, and spiritual bodies
- Assist in the body's energetic flow
- Increase one's sense of well-being
- Help release any past trauma that may be held as an energetic block to conception
- Help shift potential negative perception of oneself and one's body
- Deliver love and high vibrational energy
- Deeply relax the mind and body to assist with any anxiety of trying to get pregnant and therefore letting go of that doubt
- Place healing focus on the sacral chakra, which is said to govern the reproductive organs

Equally, I feel it can be a beneficial treatment for both partners, an expression of one's commitment to self-care that is crucial at one of life's greatest transformational times. It's easy in modern life to forget the need and importance of self-nurture throughout the process and instead get caught up in the mind and planning. In my experience, Reiki can often help shift the perspective of conception from becoming a challenging task, to regaining connection with a sense of inner strength, knowing, and trust.

Research has shown that high levels of stress can negatively affect conception and that Reiki can significantly reduce the systems of stress and anxiety by enabling the mind and body to become deeply relaxed.

Throughout pregnancy

Reiki can be a wonderful treatment and tool throughout pregnancy. In addition to the benefits listed already, it can continue to offer balance and self-care, as well as begin to build and strengthen an energetic awareness and relationship with the baby. Later in the pregnancy, Reiki can also assist with tiredness, aches, and pains, and with any anxieties that may be growing regarding the birth.

On occasions in my own pregnancy, it was overwhelming to feel the sense of responsibility to this being growing inside my body. Something that I wholly welcomed, but I also was aware that it could easily deter me from my own need for self-care. All too often, I have witnessed the beginnings of the priority shifting from mom to baby, in a way that is not always balanced or helpful. Of course, our priority as a mother is to look after our child; yet, I feel even more so is the importance of looking after yourself. Reiki can help with that balance, without having to add that on the to-do list. In a Reiki session, both mom and baby receive Reiki during pregnancy (whether that is with a Reiki practitioner or if you are trained to give yourself Reiki).

I have been privileged to hold space and offer support to many pregnant women over the years. The flow of energy and love never ceases to amaze me. Many practitioners, including myself, often report that they can distinctly feel the energy of the baby, as well as the mother: literally feeling life grow.

When I talk about holding space for a client or student, I refer to the intention of creating a safe, conscious and nonjudgmental energetic container for the individual to fully allow themselves to be held in during our time together. This maximizes the potential for them to "let go" of perceived expectation on themselves or an outcome and truly be held in the present moment, as it is.

In addition to holding sessions for clients during pregnancy, I have also had a number of students who have felt guided to take the beginnings of their Reiki training during this sacred time. All have reported a sense of well-being and empowerment for themselves, as well as a strengthened connection to their unborn child. Indeed, I know of many "Reiki rascals" who have entered the world already having had an attunement to Reiki. What a wonderful start!

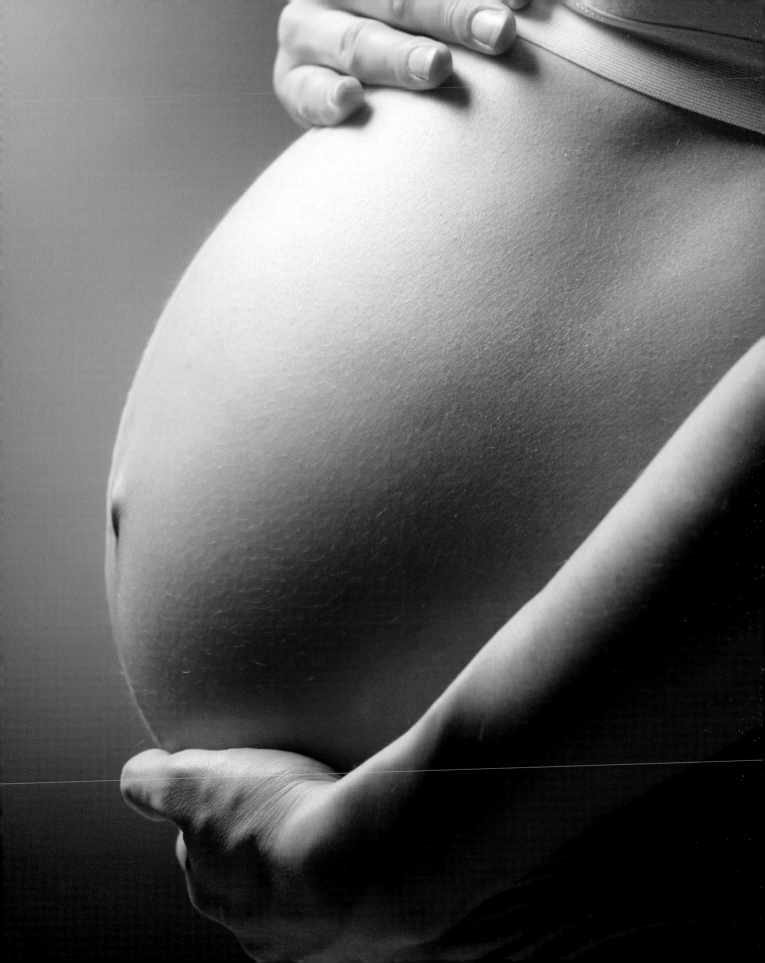

Birth and beyond

Birth for everyone is a unique experience, and I feel it is essential to honor that. For some it is a joyful, planned-out, and effortless experience, yet for others it can be deeply traumatic. Reiki can be very effective in helping to restore balance to the entire mind-body-spirit system after birth, whatever the experience. I believe that nurturing and supporting a new mother are essential ingredients for her, in turn, to nurture her infant. Of course, it isn't all about the mother. Fathers and birth partners undergo their own transitions during pregnancy, birth, and the postpartum period. They too can gain much benefit from Reiki sessions. Let's be honest—caring for a newborn can be both beautiful but draining to all involved. I feel that Reiki can help restore and balance energy levels as well as provide some much-needed serenity during this exciting and transformational time.

Babies can also benefit from Reiki sessions after childbirth, helping them to adapt to their new world. Energetically, they are very open channels to Reiki, so the time needed is greatly reduced. However, since Reiki is essentially life force energy that our body understands, recipients will receive only what they need at that time for their highest good, despite their age. I have held a Reiki session on many occasions with a baby lying on their mother's chest; it can be a beautiful experience for the mother (or father) and baby to have Reiki together.

Ultimately, I feel that as well as having sessions, each member of the family can greatly benefit from Reiki training. Reiki can become an invaluable tool to learn to harness positive energy and its benefits and can become an integral part of everyday family life from birth.

It has been proven that nurturing touch is a fundamental part of a baby's and child's well-being and development. Having an additional awareness of their energetic well-being and connection brings a beneficial and deeper level of understanding to this. As a mother with Reiki, I knew that I had a support system that I could instantly rely on and draw on at any time, both for myself and for my baby.

In addition to Reiki, learning baby massage can be of great benefit during the early months. I know it was for me. The duality of Reiki and massage, be that in a baby or an adult, can be a beautiful, relaxing, and physically beneficial combination.

Areas where Reiki may benefit a baby:

- Sleep
- Balance
- Lowering any stress the baby may be experiencing
- Help strengthen the attachment bond between parent and child
- Deeply affirming
- Relaxing for both the parent and the child

Exercise 7

Pause, breathe, smile

As a mother, I know only too well that there have been times where I can easily get overwhelmed by an event, a conversation, or even a comment involving my baby/child, which can leave me ungrounded and consequently reactive. I have learned (often the hard way) that acting from a place of reaction will generally not serve me, or the recipient. This is of course true in all aspects of our life but has been proven frequently since being a parent.

Below is a simple but effective mindfulness acronym that I use and have shared with others pretty much on a daily basis.

It can be incredibly effective in those times when we need to distance ourselves from the potential oppression of the situation and reconnect with the present moment.

It is simply this: PBS
Pause
Breathe
Smile

This gentle reminder affords us the opportunity to shift from reaction into a place of choice and can simultaneously change the energy of any given moment. A very useful tool in motherhood!

It is through our hands that we speak to the child. That we communicate. Touch is the child's first language, understanding comes long after feeling.

—Frédérick Leboyer, MD

子
child

A FRESH LOOK AT CHILDHOOD

A fresh look at childhood

I often hear people say, "I wouldn't want to be a child growing up these days." It is a tough world right now, although of course it has been tough before. I believe each generation has its own challenges; they may just be different challenges from those who have come before us.

When looking at our current society, perhaps it is obvious what the challenges are that children face today. On a global scale, we can think of climate change, war, political unrest, pandemics; on a microscale, perhaps it's social media pressures and screen time. To be honest, the list is endless.

Yet, scratch beneath the surface of our new generation and I feel a true resilience: a sensitivity, hope, and awareness that will help them rise above these challenges and flourish. I believe it is this element of our youth that is essential to nurture and hold through the turbulence, since like us, they have the answers within.

I have always been drawn to introduce Reiki to children, since not only are they often curious, but they simply get it. Children tend not to have the countless layers of culturally influenced behaviors and beliefs that adults carry. They are clearer channels. That is, until (for the majority of children) they go to school and are placed in a system that, for the most part, neither has the time nor the capacity to hold this space of development. This is not meant to be a judgment on the education system, just an observation and sadness that is an inevitable truth.

I remember going through the same process myself as a child. I see now that as a young child, I was acutely aware of energies and a more conscious way of life, yet often that was (and still is) viewed as weird. Unfortunately, after a while children believe what is said of them, and naturally turn their awareness down, or even off, in order to fit in and to be accepted. I grew up in a generation that freely used the phrase "Children are to be seen and not heard." The energy of this statement sticks and has consequently taken me years to unlearn. That is just one example; I'm sure we all have lots. I meet many early-sewn beliefs in my client work, when as adults they have come to a point where those early beliefs are now causing huge blocks in their ability to grow in their life, their families, their careers, and, importantly, themselves.

What if there's a different way? Not to wait until those blocks are so ingrained that it can take years to clear.

I believe we have the opportunity to support children in their innate connection to themselves, nature, and Source from an early age. To hold space for them to grow their emotional intelligence and awareness safely and still encourage them to be kids. There is time: this is the time.

Technology has changed our world forever; some would say for the better, but others would not agree. I feel it is wasted energy trying to undo what is done and to fight against the inevitable challenges our children face, but instead to seek ways to bring balance and empowerment to kids through their childhood.

We live in an age where labeling children with a condition to explain their behavior has become a normal and often-necessary route in order to get support. Of course, I encourage accessibility to support for children (and parents), whether that be at home or in school. However, I feel it is equally important to ensure that the labels placed on children do not define or potentially limit them. I feel that equal support can be offered by truly listening and seeing them as they are, and as always coming back to ourselves and our own healing path, since often children are our direct mirrors.

"Reiki rascals" has been a term that I have used for many years to relate to my work with Reiki and children. Jackie Rees and I used to run classes for youngsters back in the first few years of the 2000s. Yet, it was the birth of my son that truly ignited my passion to offer children support and energetic exploration through Reiki and mindfulness. Arthur is now ten and has always been a highly sensitive old soul. I used to find him talking to my late grandad when he was around three. It is no surprise that I was guided to attune him at the age of five years old, and that he is very much on his own individual journey. He continues to be my teacher and guide, as many children are, and I am grateful to be his mother, every second of the day.

As with many other children, Arthur's awareness and sensitivity do not come without challenge. However, my hope is that by sharing these holistic tools with children, they have some chance of not "turning it all off," but harnessing that beauty and connection to their true self, their childhood, and one day their purpose.

I am often asked, "At what age can my child learn Reiki?" First, I think it's really important that the curiosity in learning Reiki is led from the child and not forced in any way. I also feel that it is important for at least one of the parents to be Reiki trained, in order to have awareness of how to energetically support their child on their journey. Over the years, I have tended to teach in a two-tiered approach, five-to-eleven-year-olds and twelve-to-sixteen-year-olds, since the two age groups often have different needs. However, of course, every child is different. Children understand that Reiki is love, and it is always a truly humbling experience to hold a class and witness their natural wisdom unfold. Authenticity is key, since children (even more so than adults) will see straight through any teacher but equally will be open to receive what is being shared.

Energetic exploration can start at any age. I used to hold an hour's toddler class where we would explore energy through sound, color, and play. I have great memories of encouraged mess, noise, and fun! Recently, I have been working with more and more teenagers, who are feeling lost, anxious, and often ungrounded as they try to navigate a disconnected world of pressure, exposure, and demands. Often, just a safe space to fully express themselves without judgment is the starting point. Reiki, mindfulness practice, and simply being seen and heard can then support further healing. Learning to accept emotions for what they are—rather than letting them define you—is key to our well-being at any age, as is our empowerment of knowing we have the tools to help ourselves in challenging times.

When I first met Sam, I was ridden with anxiety and very unhappy. Being a fifteen-year-old boy, I felt a bit uncomfortable talking about my life and well-being, as it's not a subject that came up much. During my sessions with Sam, she has helped me tackle my problems in the most diplomatic but effective way possible. Sometimes I think what my life would be like now if I hadn't met Sam and continued our sessions, and it's crazy to think what it would've turned out to be and what paths I might have taken. If you have already started seeing Sam (or are thinking about it), my advice to you would be to be as open as possible even though at times it will be hard. Trust me.

—*Samuel*

Finding Ray's Key

Back in 2018, I published my first book, called *Finding Ray's Key* (a play on the words "finding Reiki").

Ray is based on Arthur, and when I initially wrote the book, it became apparent that it was to honor three very different aspects of my life: my son, my late mum, and my Reiki. I felt strongly guided to begin to share my feelings through the written word. How Reiki and mindfulness could help children (and adults) find a way to connect to their sensitivity and the idea of happiness, through safe, mindful exploration. To address the fact that we are not alone in our feelings, that all of us have "clouds," and that all emotions are important. Yet, honoring that we also have choice, a voice, and a strength within and around us that we can nourish and connect to.

The universal question of "What is the key to being happy?" that rang so true with Arthur, with my mother, and with the reasons that I was called to Reiki and mindfulness over twenty years ago quite effortlessly became the thread of the book. Since its publication, I have been invited to visit many schools, groups, and libraries to share its message. I am so grateful that *Finding Ray's Key* has become, for many, a way in for discussion about energy, mindfulness, connection, and the importance of fostering emotional intelligence from a young age.

A little exercise with a lot of depth—grow your own happy list

Take some time to create a list of things that make you happy. Keep it safe and add to it whenever you can. Simply taking the time to sit down with your children and make space for this exploration can bring about a welcome emotional shift. By engaging in this exercise alongside our children, it can reinforce the importance of the wish for us to be happy throughout our life. Often, remembering what makes us happy can effortlessly help us to move toward it.

Pebble meditation for children

This is a beautiful meditation that I often use with children. It was created by renowned Zen master, poet, and peace activist Thich Nhat Hanh. He devised this meditation as a way for children to experience meditation and learn about certain qualities within us all. Each of the four pebbles used in the meditation represents an object and its corresponding qualities. These are

- A flower—the qualities of freshness, beauty, and joy
- A mountain—the qualities of solidity, strength, and confidence
- Still water—the qualities of reflection, calm, and focus
- Space—the qualities of freedom, happiness, and peace.

Each time I hold this meditation it is slightly different, depending on the child and whatever words feel most appropriate at the time. You'll know what is best in your own situation. If possible, I like to first invite the child to choose four pebbles that they would like to use during the meditation (and afterward keep). This instantly empowers the child to be present in their choice and connection to these objects of nature.

The first pebble (flower):

I then ask them to sit in a comfortable position, perhaps cross-legged, and to place the pebbles on their left-hand side. After a few slow-guided breaths, I invite them to pick up the first pebble (which represents a flower) with their left hand and look at it with open eyes and an open heart. Then cup it with the right hand and repeat these words:

Breathing in, I see myself as a flower
Breathing out, I feel fresh
Flower, Fresh

Take a few breaths together and then invite the child to be curious about how it feels to feel fresh in their body. When ready, place the pebble down on their right-hand side.

The second pebble (mountain):

Then on to the second pebble (mountain), with the same process but with these words:

Breathing in, I see myself as a mountain
Breathing out, I feel solid
Mountain, Solid

The third pebble (still water):

Breathing in, I see myself as still water
Breathing out, I see things as they truly are
Water, Reflecting

The fourth pebble (space):

Breathing in, I see myself as space
Breathing out, I feel free
Space, Free

To close, bring your hands together in front of your heart, lower your head, and say a few words of gratitude. Alternatively, perhaps you may have a bell to ring or simply invite whoever is practicing to end on a smile.

OUR BEAUTIFUL PLANET

Our beautiful planet

Mother Earth, Gaia, Our Planet—
however we choose to refer to the
beautiful world in which we abide,
I believe that now more than ever,
it is imperative that we deepen our
relationship with her. Reiki, as you might
imagine, can be a magnificent way of
doing this. Just as Reiki assists us in
deepening our connection with self and
others, without doubt, it also enables us
to deepen our connection with all that
is. When I say all, I refer to the animals,
the plants, the trees, the water, the
soil, and fundamentally the undeniable
energetic web between us.

Our well-being is intrinsically linked with nature, yet so often in
modern society we do not take the time to feel that connection
in any depth. In fact, for many people there seems to be a sense
of complacency that accompanies our cohabiting of the planet.
The opportunity to awaken to the tangible beauty of our Earth
is available to us every day through energetic, mindful, and
compassionate living. The more we open our eyes and heart
to this opportunity, the greater benefit it will have on our entire
ecosystem. We are not separate: we are one and our actions
have consequences.

Of course, this is not new thinking, and I'm constantly heartened and inspired by the numerous individuals, of all ages, who are taking a stand and bringing their truth about the planet, its inhabitants, and the crucial shift back to living in equilibrium. It may not be possible, or even useful, for us all to take on the world in a public way. However, I feel it is essential that we all play our part in nurturing our relationship with the planet in whichever way we can. This nurturing grows with energetic awareness. Not only to casually observe but to truly see and feel the world around us. Perhaps that is grown through how we interact with animals, what we choose to consume, how we connect with and learn from nature. Reiki can help heighten our awareness, and through daily practice and being present, we are able to reconnect with our roots and, if you like, the Shaman within.

The opportunity to experience Reiki with animals, food, water, plants, trees—in fact, anything we should be guided toward—has always been a magical part of this journey. By no means is Reiki limited to working with humans. After taking Reiki I, it has often been my experience that students are effortlessly drawn to experiment with their Reiki in the natural world. I encourage students to Reiki their plants if they appear to need some nurturing, and to note their growth. To Reiki their water and food, and to note any difference in taste and consumption; to head out into the woods and to mindfully listen to the sound of the birdsong, the wind; to spend time with trees; to notice the insects underfoot, the hidden fungi, and the essence of the forest on their breath. This is truly living with Reiki, when it allows our perception of the world to widen and narrow, within the same instance: to connect with the heartbeat of living vibration.

Animal Reiki

Many people are drawn to Reiki because of its healing benefit to animals, as well as humans. For some, this is a wish to simply feel empowered to help a family pet or an injured bird, or to connect to a neighborly horse. Others may be called to pursue a professional career in animal Reiki. There has been an increase in the popularity of animal Reiki over the past decade or so. Consequently, it is becoming commonplace in many animal sanctuaries and veterinary practices, as well as in the home. In many countries, animal Reiki has become a recognized and stand-alone modality. For those wishing to work in professional practice, there are now specific animal Reiki courses available. These often include in-depth training around animal psychology, anatomy, and physiology, as well as industry guidelines and requirements.

Some of the benefits of animal Reiki:

- Relaxation, which, as with humans, naturally allows the body to reach an optimum state of healing itself, be that from illness, injury, or other stress to the body
- It can bring about greater comfort and improved well-being
- It may help with behavioral issues
- **It can assist in a peaceful end-of-life transition**
- Typically, animal Reiki is carried out in the animal's familiar surroundings and so is less stressful
- As with human Reiki, the treatment is complementary to conventional medicine
- It is nondiagnostic, noninvasive, and nonmanipulative

At its core, any animal Reiki is a privileged opportunity to connect with an animal at a heart-sense level. Similarly to children, they have an open, clear, and sensitive understanding of energy and therefore can instantly feel any lack of sincerity or the input of ego. Usually, any formal session is animal led, with cues, expression, and behavior closely monitored and read by the practitioner. Yet, a similar respect and understanding is called for whether working on a family pet, an animal in a zoo, or a butterfly that may land on your window. Animals have much to teach us, and we have much to learn.

Reiki and water

For many years, I have been fascinated by water and its vitality. In particular, by appreciating the fact that both the human body and our planet are made up of approximately 70 percent water by volume. However, it was not until I was introduced to the work of Dr. Masaru Emoto that I was able to see how my appreciation of water could actually have an energetic impact. Put another way, how the energy of our thoughts and feelings toward water can influence its molecular structure.

I was already in no doubt, after years of my own experimenting, that after I had given Reiki to a glass of water it would taste better. However, Dr. Emoto spent his life researching the impact of energetic influences on water. His work led him to extensive research in exposing water to different vibrations which included music, images and the energy of our conscious intent through our thoughts, words and prayers. He developed a process to reveal the energetic qualities and changes within the molecular structure of water through freezing it into ice crystals after consciously exposing the water to differing vibrations and observing any change in its appearance.

His findings were remarkable and showed how water can be influenced by conscious intent and linked to the dynamics of human consciousness. His findings have inspired millions including scientists to pursue a deeper understanding of water.

Later in his life, it became his mission to share this information with every child on the planet by announcing it at the UN Headquarters at a seminar he gave in 2005 via gifting his book 'The Messages from Water', Children's Version. Sadly, Dr. Emoto passed over in 2014, but his work and legacy are continued through the Emoto Peace Project, a non-profit organisation that I am honored to represent in the Southwest of England.

The book continues to be distributed to fulfil this mission (I often gift it in my Reiki classes). It is hoped The Message from Water for Children will help teach children about their own true nature as water-based beings; hence keeping themselves happy and healthy from childhood, through their teens and into their adulthood by holding reverence for water within their own bodies and for all water on the planet. Something that I believe is fundamental to our future.

Reiki and drumming

One way in which I love to connect with Mother Earth and nature is through my drum. Reiki Drumming™ was introduced as a Reiki technique by Michael Arthur Baird in the US in 1999. The technique beautifully combines Reiki, sound healing, and shamanic practice and allows us to connect with the ancient wisdom within, be that in nature or while channeling for another.

Of course, drums have been used by cultures all over the world throughout history for healing, meditation, and sacred rituals. They provide the perfect tool of connection with the divine and with Mother Earth. In professional practice, a practitioner uses the drum to assist in introducing Reiki energy into a person's energy field. This can enhance and encourage a state of deep relaxation and release any tensions, reminding the body of its optimal vibration. However, the drum can be used to connect with the elements, the directions, Mother Earth, or Father Sky. It can also be a wonderful tool of self-expression, as well as assisting in journeying. For many, it offers an innate knowing of times gone by, as we consciously connect in the present.

Exercise 9
Forest bathing

Time to take a mindful trip to the forest?

For many, being out in nature is a direct route to feeling more grounded and calmer. The term "forest bathing" relates to a Japanese practice of relaxation known as shinrin yoku. It is the practice of being mindful among trees, observing both the breath and the surrounding nature to enhance relaxation and well-being.

Whether you refer to it as Reiki, bathing, or being mindful in the forest, the intention is to tap into the supportive energy around you. In addition, it can be a beautiful practice to introduce a mantra to your mindful walk.

These are some simple guidelines for your forest experience:

- Choose a time and destination where you will be at ease and not rushed.
- Begin by being suitably dressed for comfort and temperature, and switching your phone off.
- As you start your walk, make a conscious note of your speed and see if it's possible to slow your pace down.
- Begin to notice your breath, and when you are ready, allow yourself to take some longer, deeper breaths deep into the belly, and in turn extending the exhalation while softening the shoulders.

- After a while, stop walking: stand still or sit down for a moment.
- First, what you can smell? Then extend your curiosity into what you can see, hear, and touch. Fully absorb your surroundings by using all of your senses.
- If you notice your mind starting to wander, be kind to yourself and gently bring your focus back to your curiosity and observations.
- Stay as long as you feel guided with your eyes open, absorbing the natural colors of the forest.
- If you wish, you may want to take another stroll, this time at an even-slower pace. Take note of how your feet feel each time they touch the ground. How your feet feel in your shoes, the sound of your feet on the path, the sensations felt on each step. As you do so, you may wish to chant the mantra *I am home. I am safe.*
- Continue your mindful walk for as long as you are comfortable before again finding a suitable space to sit down and just "be" in the forest.

It is thought that two hours is an optimum time for a complete forest-bathing experience, but as always, I feel ten minutes is better than nothing. So be kind to yourself and perhaps build up your practice as time and inclination allow.

IF ANYTHING,
BE KIND

If anything, be kind

If you can be anything in life:

First, be kind

Second, be kind

Third, be kind

Kindness to all beings has always come fairly naturally to me. I am often referred to as having a big heart. I do have a big heart, and I'm proud of that. However, genuine kindness to myself has been far more of a challenging journey (and continues to be a work in progress). I feel it is no coincidence that when I first began my Reiki journey and was introduced to the Reiki principles, the last precept was relayed as "Just for today, be kind to yourself as well as others." This instantly resonated with me, and I was intrigued to discover only later that the "kind to yourself" element was not included in the original precepts. I, however, still choose to include this element, since I feel it beautifully reinforces Usui Sensei's invitation that Reiki is, in the first instance, a pathway of spiritual growth of self. I have come to understand that unless I can truly be kind to myself, there will always be a limit to my ability to serve others, since eventually I will inevitably fall over. Perhaps a more clinical term to describe this would be to experience compassion fatigue.

Over the years, I have noticed that I'm not alone in this, and it is seemingly a common thread among people who are guided to learn Reiki (or indeed are guided to any caring profession). One of the main reasons I hear behind students wanting to learn Reiki is to help people. This is obviously a wonderful intention. However, when asked the question "Where are you on your priority list?," often it's met with a gulp, a drop of the head, and

a recognition that they are somewhere near the bottom. In addition, there is often the consequent realization of a heavily engrained, daily habit and ease of putting others first— ignoring one's own needs and rejecting self-kindness. Of course, there are often numerous historical and often childhood factors that have led to this belief. My intention in putting the question to my students (and regularly to myself) is not to be in judgment, but to shine a crucial light of awareness.

In Reiki, as well as many other Eastern spiritual practices, there is a strong call to cultivate self-love. Within the first level of Reiki teaching, students are taught how to channel Reiki for themselves and to practice self-healing. This is then encouraged to become a daily practice and is actually fundamental to the continuation of our Reiki journey. This invitation is constant, since self-healing is a vital element of our growth path and something we are continually encouraged to return to.

In some systems of Reiki there are specific hand placements that are taught for self-treatment. Others may suggest following the chakra line with an intention of balance. Usui Reiki invites the student to cultivate trust in simple, intuitive, and divine guidance of the hands. Whatever technique is used, there lies beneath the invitation to wholly connect with oneself with kindness and an openness to receive divine love for our highest good.

For some this can be very challenging. It often involves establishing a new relationship with self-love and what it means to be kind to oneself. Often, students are met with their belief that it is somehow selfish or arrogant to show self-love and self-gratitude. Sadly, I feel that this is a misplaced belief that we have unfortunately managed to develop in Western society.

I am continually saddened at how often I meet that belief in my client work. A belief that can be incredibly destructive and one that can easily, in turn, breed feelings of self-hatred and self-criticism, the very paradox of what is nourishing in our life.

I remember hearing a story about Sharon Salzburg (a globally renowned author and meditation teacher), who described a time when she was at a conference with the Dalai Lama. She was in the audience and asked the question "What do you think about self-hatred?" She reported that the Dalai Lama, revered leader of Tibetan Buddhism, looked confused and spent a number of minutes in discussion with his translator. Eventually, he turned back to her and said, "Self-hatred . . . what is that?"

I smile at the thought of a world where this answer was commonplace.

I feel that by connecting to Reiki (personally and within our families), we can learn to be kind to ourselves and cultivate that kindness. In turn, our kindness for others can only grow and will have a ripple effect that will continue to spread. Kindness grows kindness. It is indeed about the only thing in the world that when you share it, it doubles. This fact is backed not only by our experience but by science. If you are kind to yourself, you are more likely to be kind to others. If you receive an act of kindness, then you are more likely to give an active of kindness.

Studies have shown that if we perform just one random act of kindness a day, it ultimately leads to a reduction in stress, anxiety, and any depression we may have. Our bodies are actually flooded with hormones that make us calmer, happier, and healthier. In beautiful equilibrium, the body of the person we are being kind to also has the same response. This is equally important for children and adults—whether in schools, in the home, or in the workplace. With social media now being the nucleus of communication for the majority of our youth, it is essential that we universally encourage a culture of kindness, respect, and equality. Today, we are blessed to have increasing numbers of organizations, charities, and individuals focused on the importance of kindness and compassion in many different settings. We recognize this essential human quality as a beacon for change. I have noted a few such groups in the resource section of this book, and should you feel inspired, I would encourage you to have a look at some of the wonderful tools, support, research, and wisdom available today on this subject.

As well as Reiki, we can of course use crystals, mindfulness, and plain gesture to connect to the vibration of kindness. A simple but effective tool in my home is the "thinking-of-you tray." This is just some kind of tray that is placed in a noticeable position within the home, where any member of the family is invited to leave a gift of kindness for another member. This may be a note, a flower, a chocolate bar, a drawing . . . anything that indicates that the receiver has been in the thoughts of another. It truly is a heartwarming exercise both for the person leaving the offering and to the receiver, and one that can bring about a great deal of joy.

Crystals can be another way of connecting to the intention of kindness and self-love. Rose quartz is one of the most popular crystals for this and is often referred to as the stone of universal love. It is said that rose quartz helps purify and open the heart on all levels to promote self-love and love of others, and encourages feelings of deep peace and inner healing. It can help restore balance, trust, and harmony within our lives, our home, and our hearts.

I often place rose quartz around my home to invite a sense of balance and harmony. I sometimes place a piece under my pillow or in my pocket at times when I feel disconnected or upset. Even simply sitting with a chunk of rose quartz can be enough to calm an otherwise chaotic day.

Exercise 10
The loving-kindness meditation

There are many different versions of this popular meditation, many of which have their roots based in Buddhist tradition. The focus of the meditation is to cultivate loving energy and awareness toward oneself and others by stating chosen kind intentions. With practice the meditation can extend to sending the same energy toward people with whom we have conflict or find difficult, increasing our capacity for forgiveness and acceptance.

How to practice:

1. Begin by carving out some time to practice and offer yourself this space of honoring. Turn off your phone.

2. Find a comfortable seated position and close your eyes, bringing your awareness to your breath.

3. Allow your breath to guide you into the present moment and just notice your natural in-and-out flow of breath, allowing the body and mind to quiet with each exhalation.

4. When you feel ready, gently bring awareness to yourself in this moment and recognize the fact that you wish to be happy, well, and accepting of yourself just as you are. Consciously offer yourself these phrases:

May I be happy.
May I be well.
May I be free from suffering.
May I be safe.
May I live my life with ease.

5. Enjoy immersing yourself in these intentions, allowing the warmth and energy of these words to fully embrace your presence. Let the feelings engulf you. If you find this challenging or discover your mind wandering, gently guide it back to your breath and the accompanying sensations within your body, before returning to your intentions.

6. As you practice, breathe in the feelings of love and breathe out any tension or resistance.

7. Initially this can be the entire meditation.

8. If you wish to continue, gently release the focus of yourself and bring to mind a friend or loved one and offer them the same intention and phrases. You may wish to visualize the person sitting in front of you or perhaps holding their hand. Allow yourself to feel a sense of gratitude for this person in your life, while again offering these phrases:

May you be happy.
May you be well.
May you be free from suffering.
May you be safe.
May you live your life with ease.

9. Again, if you wish to extend the meditation, you can continue with the same process and offerings, perhaps to a neighbor, a stranger, or even further, to all sentient beings. As you become familiar and confident with the practice, you may choose to include a person with whom you have difficulty, in order to find a space of forgiveness and peace.

10. When you feel guided to complete your meditation, slowly focus on the breath once more. As you begin to reorient, remind yourself of the kindness felt within your practice.

11. Take a deep breath of gratitude and recognition that this is a space you can return to whenever you choose.

礼

gratitude

CULTIVATING GRATITUDE

Cultivating gratitude

Let's face it, sometimes life is tough—there is no getting away from that. We live in a world that is fast paced, demanding, controversial, and contradictory; I could go on. It is therefore easy, and very common, to get caught up in the challenges of life. In turn, that disgruntled voice that we all recognize can become the voice that we hear above anything else. However, energetically we know that if we continue to focus on the hardships in life, we can all too easily get lost in this story and lose sight of the wonder of life.

I have learned over the years that one of the most empowering and powerful tools we have in our life is gratitude. The words "thank you" can literally be a game changer. It may sound obvious, but simply paying attention to what we are grateful for on a daily basis can help shift the weight we often carry, but more importantly wake us up to the true beauty of the planet, ourselves, and humanity. Truly recognizing how much we have to be grateful for not only is humbling but allows us to come away from our ego-driven thoughts and constant striving or despair and allows us to fully live in the moment with love and connection.

Cultivating gratitude is therefore a vital skill in our well-being and the well-being of our planet. It may sound simple, but like all of our work, it takes time and practice. Gratitude is something that most of us can cognitively understand with ease, but the magic is in its embodied state of our being, where it becomes a natural pathway for ourselves and consequently for others.

Gratitude is a fundamental and beautiful part of Reiki practice. Whether it is during self-healing, working with others, Reiki shares, or distance healing, there is always the element of gratitude within the process. Gratitude can be shown in a number of forms during our practice. First, by when we place our hands in what is known in Reiki as gasshô (hands together in front of the heart). This physical gesture brings with it the energy of presence, ancient wisdom, connection, and clear intention as we state our wish to either begin or end our practice with thanks.

In addition to the hands being in gasshô, gratitude is also offered in verbal form during practice, either audibly or spoken in the mind. Commonly, this is where we state our thanks for connection to Source and for the Reiki energy/healing that has been received, and also for any guidance that we may receive through our work and lineage.

On a core level, gratitude is offered as one of the daily Reiki principles: "Just for today, I will be grateful." It was therefore Mikao Usui's invitation for all students of Reiki to focus on gratitude as a daily practice. It has been my experience that having a daily sense of gratitude and noncomplacency is one of the key factors that strengthens our integrity and Reiki practice, as well as everyday living.

There are of course many ways in which we can bring gratitude into our daily lives and our home. I wanted to share a few, the energy of which has served both myself and my family and helped us connect to this vital component of healthy living on a daily basis.

A grateful heart is a magnet

for miracles

—Anonymous

Gratitude jars

This is a beautiful daily or weekly ritual that can be introduced to the family at the dinner table. The idea is simply to take a moment each evening, perhaps after you have finished a meal, to find some time and space for each member of the family to write down on a piece of paper something that they are grateful for. This is then kept secret, with the piece of paper folded and placed directly into a designated gratitude jar. Of course, the jar can be anything, but it's nice for it to be glass so that the family can see the jar filling up as the days/weeks go on. The family can then decide a suitable day and time in which the jar will be opened and shared. The awareness of gratitude can be anything from a flower seen that day, to a smile received or a call from a friend, to being grateful for the food on the table. Whatever comes to mind can be written down. It is important to ensure that the ritual is kept fun and simple and without judgment of what is written, but wholly accepting of whatever it is that comes to mind in that moment.

A gratitude journal

This again is a simple daily ritual that can really help bring perspective and positive closure to any day. By one having some kind of journal by the bed, the intention is to make the last thing you do before sleeping a space to bring to mind three things that you are grateful for from the day. Some days this might be easier than others, but it is important to be kind to yourself if you are struggling, and not to bring judgment to that feeling. It can be helpful on the tough days to keep it simple and offer acceptance to that need.

Exercise 11
Meditation of gratitude

As I mentioned earlier, the magic in gratitude can be enhanced when we fully allow ourselves to feel the emotion of gratitude within the body. This short meditation can allow the opportunity to drop into that space and begin to cultivate the attitude of gratitude within us. You may wish to record these words or just read them through a few times before guiding yourself into the meditation.

1. As always, you begin by turning off your phone, ensuring you have some uninterrupted time, and finding a comfortable position to sit or lie in.

2. Then close your eyes and take a couple of deep breaths, as you begin to allow your body to settle and your mind to calm.

3. Perhaps just rest the awareness on the breath for a few rounds and observe the natural inflow and outflow of breath.

4. With each exhalation, imagine your body softening and becoming heavier as you begin to fully connect with the moment and allow the body to relax.

5. Continue focusing on your breath but now expand that focus to include your whole body lying or sitting in this space. Become aware of a soft and golden light spreading from the crown of your head and flowing down through the body and surrounding you, offering warmth and protection as you drop into this space of love and connection.

6. On your next inhalation, gently bring to mind something or someone that you are grateful for—it could be a loved one, a meal that you've had today, a pet, a compliment you received at work, a smile—whatever comes to mind, see if you can lightly allow it to rest in your consciousness.

7. As you do so, breathe, pause, and say the words "thank you" to whatever it is. Perhaps you are visualizing a person and can tell them how grateful you are for them and why. Perhaps it is a beautiful flower you saw earlier. Whatever is in your heart, see if it's possible to offer those simple and powerful words: "thank you."

8. As you continue to breathe and enjoy the space, you may wish to let whatever is in your mind fade, and to bring something else in that you are grateful for, again offering the words "thank you."

9. If you are having trouble bringing something into your mind, just notice that in this moment and offer yourself some kindness without any judgment, gently bringing your awareness back to your breath again to anchor yourself once more, and then maybe bringing into mind a part of your body you are grateful for. Perhaps your eyes, your ears, your hands . . . whatever feels right for you; our bodies offer us so much on a daily basis.

10. Now see if you can feel this sense of gratitude within your body. Perhaps it's revealing itself as a warmth, a sensation, a color . . . again, whatever is with you, just noticing and allowing that pleasant feeling to spread throughout your body. Enjoy how your sense of gratitude is washing away any tension or negativity that may be within you. Know that this is a place you can revisit and grow.

11. As you feel the meditation coming to an end, you may wish to gently drop in the following words: *"Thank you for my many blessings. May I accept these blessings with ease and grace as I continue to notice and give thanks for them."*

12. When you are ready, slowly bring your awareness back to your breath and gently open your eyes.

声
voice

DON'T JUST TAKE MY WORD FOR IT

Don't just take my word for it

No doubt it is clear by now that I am passionate about Reiki and energy work. Consequently, I am conscious that some might say that I am somewhat biased in my relaying of its benefits. Therefore, I felt it important to include within these pages some personal feelings of insight and experience of others who have chosen to have Reiki in their life.

The individuals I asked to contribute are a cross section of people whom I have been blessed to meet as students, clients, teachers, and friends, many of whom have become Reiki masters themselves. I asked each of them if they would write a short piece to share their feelings about how receiving, learning, or teaching Reiki has influenced their life—whether in general or during a specific time or event. It is with deep gratitude and humility that I am able to share their words with you.

"I think I have known about Reiki since I was quite young, but I didn't have a name for it in those days. I've always been an emotional person, which often led me to being reactive. During my teens, I would react to my mother telling me off as I left the house to see my friends. I would choose to start a verbal fight, which would inevitably leave me upset, late, and arriving at my friend's house in a bad mood. Sometimes it would last the entire evening. I believe I found Reiki through wanting to change that reactive part of myself.

"This intention for change first led me to learn how to breathe consciously and to leave my mind as empty as possible. To be able to watch my emotions from the outside without judgment and just let them be, accepting them as they were. I realize I wasn't conscious all of the time, but I was trying to accept myself. As a direct consequence of this act, those negative emotions started to fade away; I was raising my vibration, and I was controlling my own energy flow.

"Sam appeared in my life at the most perfect time, like all good things in life. She helped me to understand what Reiki is and to accept myself and my actions; I started practicing. I practiced in an empowered and pure way, being able to access the most-beautiful places of my heart. I realized the more love and kindness I spread in the world, the stronger it was reciprocated when I needed it the most (not when I thought I needed it, which is a completely different thing).

"I started incorporating Reiki as my part of my daily routine. Last thing at night, first thing in the morning. I made sure that most days I was spending at least five minutes channeling Reiki. Sometimes it was to myself, other times to other people or situations. In the last seven years I think I've basically Reiki'd everything around me (just the thought of it makes me smile). From the food I cook, to the patients I treat (I am a dentist), to the breast milk that my daughter had for more than the first two years of her life. I also loved to Reiki my dog and found it invaluable when he was ill.

"One time I feel it is important to share is when I was guided to work on my husband, who was suffering from a very strong pain in his back. I had literally just returned from a workshop weekend where I had been practicing energy channeling. Due to his pain, I held a very long and what felt like an intense Reiki session. It was probably the most intense session we'd experienced during our relationship. It just happened that way. Feeling very relieved, he said it was a perfect day for a walk in the forest, as the fall was just showing. He drove us to a beautiful forest half an hour away from home. Once in the forest and after a three-minute walk, he felt a very strong pain in his chest and collapsed in front of my shocked eyes. By coincidence (or maybe not), a cardiologist and his friend who was an anesthesiologist were walking 20 meters away from us, and they saved his life after forty-five minutes of CPR. What gave him the strength and the clarity to take us to that forest prior to that event? I've chosen to believe in Reiki and what resonates with me, and I feel because of this we were able to go on and have the most wonderful three-year-old daughter."

Aynoa, 37, dentist (trained to Reiki master practitioner)

"Reiki is a grounding and an uplifting force in my life. This sounds contradictory, but I feel rooted while at the same time, more aware and in tune with the steps I am taking in life to grow. It has helped enormously with feeling connected. This may sound airy . . . so to pin it down . . . I feel Reiki sessions helped with recognizing when I was caught in my head, like a hamster in a wheel, through to a space that exists around thoughts. I am more present of late in this spaciousness and feel a guidance here. Reiki has helped me trust this guidance, even in times when there seems (to my hamster mind) to be no discernible light or logic! Reiki work has helped me make changes in my life and to accept situations so they can begin to change. Reiki is a constant in a changing world and, as the serenity prayer puts it, grants me 'the serenity to accept the things I cannot change, courage to change the things I can, and wisdom to know the difference.'"

Adrian, 46, SENDCo teacher (trained to Reiki level II)

"By opening the door to Reiki, it allowed everything around me to be touched. My relationship with myself, with others, my sense of belonging. Finding purpose and feeling fulfilled. A state of balance and harmony.

"I feel Reiki enables us to journey into our past, our future; to revisit the times when we have been hurt and to send some healing. Such a wonderful way to learn and to grow. Manifesting our potential. As we do so we can start to open up and to forgive. And sometimes it is hard, and it takes time. So, whilst we wait for the storm to pass, we can turn to Reiki to fill us with light, with love. So much love . . . Like a river running wild that cannot be contained. We can then choose to let go of all the walls we have built around us, to allow our vibrations to be raised. To stand tall for the world to come closer. We can feel quite vulnerable being so open, but as we hold our hands out, the magic begins.

"As a Reiki Master Teacher and Practitioner as well as being on my own Reiki journey, I have encountered wonderful healing, both of myself and of others. Being attuned to Reiki was a unique experience and for many, it feels like receiving a new set of lenses to better see the world we live in.

"Reiki has always been present for me in all the moments of doubt. A guide on my path. Enabling us to transform and to go back to the simplicity of life. The small things that mean the world to us. Reiki is a wonderful gift, offering a journey of possibilities, and so much more."

Céline, 36, Language & Yoga Teacher (a Reiki Master Teacher at the Devon School of Reiki)

"After an incredibly challenging number of years at work due to unprecedented and traumatic circumstances, I had reached a point where I could not take much more. I was in unknown territory—I felt alone, uncertain and suffering physically and mentally. A colleague suggested I should see Sam, a Reiki therapist."

"The first meeting was amazing. Surrounded by strange objects, brass bowls, crystals—even a drum and a couch, I knew that I was totally out of my comfort zone. Sam knew that too—she also knew (she told me later) that I was totally skeptical. We just talked. Or rather I talked. Sam guided me to face up to who I was and what I could and could not control in my life."

"Throughout this period in my life I can honestly say that Reiki not only kept me going, it rebuilt me and gave me tools to cope in seemingly overwhelming circumstances. I drew on a strength I never knew I had, not over-confident but authentic and giving myself the space to speak my truth in incredibly stressful situations. Those who were witness to these changes, could not believe I was so seemingly calm."

"Beyond that period of extreme stress at work, I continue to attend Reiki sessions, and always will. It has made me a more effective leader and colleague and, more importantly, a better father to my children. It has made me value the moment and find happiness in the seemingly smallest of things, a bird singing, a leaf on a tree or an achievement by someone I hardly know."

"As I grow older, I really am becoming wiser, not from the things I have achieved, more from an appreciation of self and an inward abundance of 'life energy.' A calmness and grounding I have never had before. Reiki has made me a better person."

John, 60, company CEO (a Reiki client)

"My healing and Reiki journey started one dull November evening in 1995. I had been working in London for several years and was plagued by constant back pain, anxiety, tiredness, and the knowledge that something was missing in my life. Accepting an invitation from my daughter and daughter-in-law, I attended a psychic fair on that dull November evening, a decision that would ultimately change my life. Although I had heard of Reiki, I had never had a treatment and was unsure of what to expect. The treatment I had that night filled me with peace, a renewed sense of self, less pain, and the desire to know more about Reiki."

"Over the next few years my rollercoaster life calmed down as I took my Reiki I, II, and master attunements. This fueled my excitement and desire to understand the physical, mental, emotional, and spiritual aspects of this wonderful energy, leading me in turn to study anatomy, physiology, hypnotherapy, and stress counseling in order to understand and fully embrace the changes that we all go through in our journey of life. I have been blessed on my path to have worked with many people, some of whom I have taught and many who have taught me."

"Within my family, we all use Reiki. One endearing memory I have is of my husband hugging a tree for the first time and feeling the universal life force energy; this memory will stay with me forever."

"Reiki is a constant in my life and has enabled me to deal with many challenging events, including the death of my son. I feel Reiki comforts, supports, and guides us and gives us wisdom. It helps in our understanding of who we are and our place in the grand scheme of things. Through it we heal and in turn heal others physically, mentally, emotionally, and spiritually: it enables us to find our joy."

Jackie, 68 (Sam's original Reiki master)

"Over the past few years I have received many beautiful experiences with my Reiki: I cherish them all. The one I am going to share with you is a time, earlier this year, when I had to have an endoscopy.

"For a few months I had been suffering with stomach problems and weight loss, which led to lots of blood tests, scans, and medication. Despite being very mindful of my diet, eventually it was decided that I needed an endoscopy. The hospital contacted me and gave me an appointment within a week. I knew that the procedure is usually performed under sedation, as it is very unpleasant. However, I really didn't want to be sedated.

"I knew that my Reiki would strengthen, hold, and guide me through the week prior to the procedure. Each day, I walked in the countryside; tuning in to the birdsong and the pure beauty of nature surrounding me, I was feeling very relaxed and positive. In the evenings, I would give myself Reiki self-healing, gently dropping into a place of inner peace. At the end of each session I was so peaceful and had a sense of strength building deep within me. I was also blessed with deep restorative sleep.

"On the morning of my hospital appointment, I performed three rounds of Reiki moving meditation. For me, this exercise always promotes positive thoughts, boosts my confidence, and grounds me. I certainly felt in a very good place: I felt strong and incredibly calm. I checked in at the hospital, where after a few questions and routine checks, I was shown to the waiting room. It turned out to be quite a wait, two and a half hours! However, I was inside my Reiki bubble and feeling a warm glow within me. Eventually they called me through; the consultant and nurses were a little surprised and concerned to hear that I had refused sedation, but respected my wishes. It certainly felt unpleasant, but I focused on my breathing and the Reiki energies with me. I focused on staying in the present moment, I knew it would be over in thirty minutes. Surprisingly, it seemed to pass quite quickly, and once the tube was removed, I felt fine in a couple of moments.

"I know without any doubt that my Reiki held and supported me through the procedure. Not once did I feel alone or anxious. A little Reiki at bedtime that night and I drifted into a blissful sleep."

Karen, 68, gardener (trained to Reiki master)

"Reiki, for me, began as an experience of relaxation and support during pregnancy. I attended sessions with Sam from day one, as it happened.

"It was a kind of beautifully timed intervention. I had booked a session not knowing a thing about Reiki, but it had come highly recommended. I didn't know when I made the appointment that I would find out I was pregnant with my first child on that same day.

"And so began my journey.

"From then, the experience of Reiki would bring a deep sense of comfort and connection during both the blissful and the deeply uncomfortable phases of growing a new baby. Reiki helped me to feel grounded, safe, and well during pregnancy and birth. I was able to connect to my own body in a way that I perhaps hadn't done before, and importantly, to be able to care for myself too.

"Reflecting now, I find it interesting that I should have first encountered Reiki when entering the new phase of self that is motherhood. It may sound clichéd, but in growing and birthing a new life, I gave new life to myself. I have become a better nurturer of me.

"For me, Reiki is empowering. It may be received through a healing session or attunement, but it is also a means of (re)discovering one's own power: the infinite source of love, healing, and possibility that resides within us all. It is both personal and universal.

"Specifically, Reiki has helped me in managing anxiety, depression, and phases of transition and has helped me to remain grounded during times of distress and disconnection. The most beautiful part is that the more my journey has progressed, the more it has become a means of being able to support myself and others. The first time I really felt this sense of empowerment was in using Reiki to calm and dispel panic attacks. It also helped me to get my ever-wakeful baby boy to sleep—yes, really.

"You never know where such a journey will go, of course. For me it went from a Reiki session one day to a Reiki master class another, and simply Reiki every day. My son is eight years old now. And he's remarkable (of course!). I really think Reiki helped make him, and us, this way.

"Thanks to my experiences, I am now more sensitive, more intuitive, more connected, and maybe braver—and humbler—than I ever have been. It's an exciting journey."

Hannah, 40, teacher & mother (trained to Reiki master practitioner)

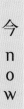

今
now

FIND YOUR KI:
IT'S TIME

Find your *ki*: It's time

It was always my intention by this
stage of the book to have shared
enough information about Reiki and
other energetic tools to have at least
sparked a growing flame of curiosity,
and at best left the reader eager to find
out the next steps.

I spoke to a potential student last night and said to him that
in my experience, one's call to Reiki may start as a quiet but
persistent knocking sound in the distance. When the time is
right, that knocking can become so loud it's as if the universe
is pounding on the very door to your soul. It's then, of course,
up to you as to whether you choose to open that door and
let the infinite light of Reiki energy flood into your life, bringing
unconditional love, support, healing, and ultimately change.

Opening the door . . .

If you find yourself in a position where that knocking is pretty
loud, then it may well be time to find your *ki*. As I detailed
earlier, there are numerous systems of Reiki to which you may
be drawn. I would always encourage a potential Reiki student
to follow their own guidance as to what feels right in terms of
both the system and their teacher. There are literally thousands
of Reiki masters in the world, I believe that if you truly listen, you
can trust that you will be guided to the right one for you.

One essential part of the puzzle is of course experiencing Reiki
for oneself, so a Reiki session is often a good place to start.

What happens in a Reiki session

Reiki sessions can often be a deeply relaxing experience where the client remains fully clothed, normally lying on a couch (or seated, if preferable), and the Reiki practitioner or master facilitates a channeling of Reiki energy by a laying on of hands. Reiki can, however, be given using a hands-off approach and working purely in the auric space (the energetic layer around the body), which some clients prefer.

I mention that it can be a relaxing experience since I feel it is important to reiterate that the client receives the necessary healing for their highest good in that moment. This cannot be predetermined, since the healing from universal life force energy is not from the practitioner but channeled from Source. Therefore, for some the healing may be a very blissful and relaxing experience; for others, it can sometimes bring about sensations within the body or a cathartic release. This is all part of the process. An invitation for the client to set an intention at the beginning of the session is often introduced to empower the client in the process of their own healing journey, thus accepting the shifts and release that are necessary.

Reiki sessions can also be held from a distance

This can be a beautiful alternative when a client is unable to leave home or if they want to work with a master who is not in their immediate vicinity. Recipients are usually fully inclusive in the process by preparing themselves and being in an open and receptive state, while the practitioner channels Reiki energy from a distance.

Reiki shares

Another wonderful way to experience Reiki with others—although most shares require participants to already be Reiki trained to at least level 1, so that participants are able to share Reiki as well as receive. Reiki shares are often the perfect opportunity to meet people on a similar path and to share and practice Reiki in a safe and held environment. Shares are often held by Reiki schools, organizations, or students, and by people who may be looking to create a Reiki community in their area. Increasingly today, Reiki shares are also held online, where a virtual space of sharing and self-practice is created.

Learning Reiki

There is usually a three- or four-level approach to learning Reiki, depending on the lineage and system you choose to study. In the more traditional lineages, each level contains an attunement (Reiju, placement, or equivalent) that I choose to refer to as a ceremony of empowerment; this determines Reiki from other spiritual practices.

There are of course many ways in which Reiki is taught in terms of time, platform, class format, content, and practice. The duration of these classes can range from a day to years, depending on lineage and system. However, in general and simple terms, the following levels are typical:

Reiki I: The First Degree (*Shoden*)

The first degree of Reiki is an introduction open to anyone, with no previous knowledge of Reiki required. It is often delivered as an experiential journey into awareness of the world of energy: how to understand and embrace the need for balance between one's physical, emotional, and spiritual bodies. The emphasis is often on self-treatment and energetic exploration.

The first level introduces working with energy and prepares the student to channel energy in a physical and practical way. This teaches each student how to work on family and friends, but most importantly, how to work on themselves. I believe that what is taught at Reiki I is very much the foundation of one's practice and journey, something to rely on and return to. Therefore, within my own classes, I am always guided to introduce the concepts (covered earlier in the book) of grounding, cleansing, and protection: the keystones of sustainable and healthy practice.

Reiki II: The Second Degree (*Okuden*)

This level encourages students to drop into a deeper level of self-healing by focusing on the heart and acknowledgment of behavioral patterns and beliefs that may no longer serve. Three Reiki symbols are shared, each with its own vibration and quality. As previously mentioned, some masters may be guided to depart the first Reiki symbol at the first degree. Completion of this class (as well as case studies with some schools) enables students to work on others and, should they choose, to set up a professional Reiki practice. Distance healing, further Reiki techniques, and meditations are also covered, with some schools including practical details of how to set up a Reiki practice and business.